The Goltermann Concerto No. 4 Study Book for Cello

Concerto by Georg Goltermann
Exercises by Cassia Harvey

CHP364

©2020 by C. Harvey Publications All Rights Reserved.

www.charveypublications.com - print books
www.learnstrings.com - downloadable books
www.harveystringarrangements.com - chamber music

Table of Contents

	Page
Movement One, Allegro Exercises	
Section One (measures 31-42)	5
Section Two (measures 43-56)	16
Section Three (measures 57-62)	22
Section Four (measures 63-77)	27
Section Five (measures 79-97a)	39
Section Six (measures 97-108)	45
Section Seven (measures 109-119)	59
About Harmonics	65
Movement Two, Andantino Exercises	Page
Section One (measures 5-40)	72
Section Two (measures 42-65a)	80
Section Three (measures 65-92)	85
Movement Three, Allegro Molto Exercises	Page
Section One (measures 13-32)	89
Section Two (measures 33-72)	91
Section Three (measures 96-112)	95
Section Four (measures 116-159)	98
Section Five (measures 160-196)	105
About Spiccato	106
Section Six (measures 217-284)	111
Section Seven (measures 308-324)	112
Section Eight (measures 328-371)	116
Section Nine (measures 372-411)	122
Section Ten (measures 412-459)	131
Complete Concerto	Page
Allegro	138
Andante	142
Allegro Molto	144

How this book works

This book divides Concerto No. 4 in G Major, by Georg Goltermann, into short sections and provides exercises for mastering each section.

Each exercise was written to teach a specific skill. Shifts are often repeated to help with acquiring muscle memory. Double stops are included for establishing relative pitch, building left-hand strength, and balancing the bow across two strings. Most of the bowing work focuses on the various slur and articulation combinations that Goltermann includes in his piece. Rhythm is often taught by subdividing longer notes into shorter beats.

Vibrato may be used throughout the book as soon as intonation is secure. Playing the exercises with vibrato will help balance the hand over the notes being played and will also help develop tone.

Roman numerals refer to strings (never positions).
I = A string
II = D string
III = G string
IV = C string

Some preparatory books and pieces to **study before** or along with this book:
- Fifth Position for the Cello: CHP198
- Learning Three-Octave Scales on the Cello (first several pages): CHP356
- Arpeggio Studies in Two Octaves for the Cello: CHP155
- The Bach Cello Suite No. 1 Study Book: CHP332
- The Romberg Sonata in C Major Study Book for Cello: CHP348

Some books and pieces to **study after** this book:
- Tenor Clef for the Cello: CHP109
- Learning Three-Octave Scales on the Cello (the rest of the book): CHP356
- Tarantella by W. H. Squire
- The Swan Study Book for Cello: CHP346
- The Faure Elegie Study Book for Cello: CHP319

Thank you for your purchase!

If you are happy with the book or have helpful information about it for other musicians and teachers, it would be super helpful if you could leave a review where you bought the book!

If you have a question about anything in this book, if there is anything you don't understand, or if there is anything you disagree with and you want to let us know, please reach out to our team at charveypublications@gmail.com; we're happy to address your issue!

If there is any defect with the printed book, please know that we ourselves do not print the books. The best way to resolve a book printing issue is to contact the company where you purchased this book (or contact us if you purchased from www.charveypublications.com) for a full refund or exchange. If you discover a defect after the return window has closed, please notify the company so they can make appropriate changes at their printing facility and then contact us at charveypublications@gmail.com so we can help you to get a correctly printed copy of the book you can use.

Above all, we want your playing and teaching experience to be better because of our books. Suggestions, ideas, criticisms and positive comments are always welcome at charveypublications@gmail.com.

We realize that paperback binding is not ideal for sheet music, however it allows us to offer this, and all of our other books, for less than half as much as we would have to charge for different binding. If you'd like a downloadable copy of this book to play from a tablet or to print out, visit www.learnstrings.com and use code printbookgoltermann to get 30% off your purchase of a PDF copy.

And visit us regularly at https://www.charveypublications.com/better-string-playing-blog for free sheet music that you might find helpful!

Here's to better string playing!

Cassia Harvey

The Goltermann Concerto No. 4 Study Book for Cello   5

Concerto, First Movement
Section One: Measures 31-42

Note: The Concerto is broken up into sections in this study book. The complete piece is at the back of the book.

Concerto No. 4 in G Major, by Georg Goltermann
Exercises by Cassia Harvey

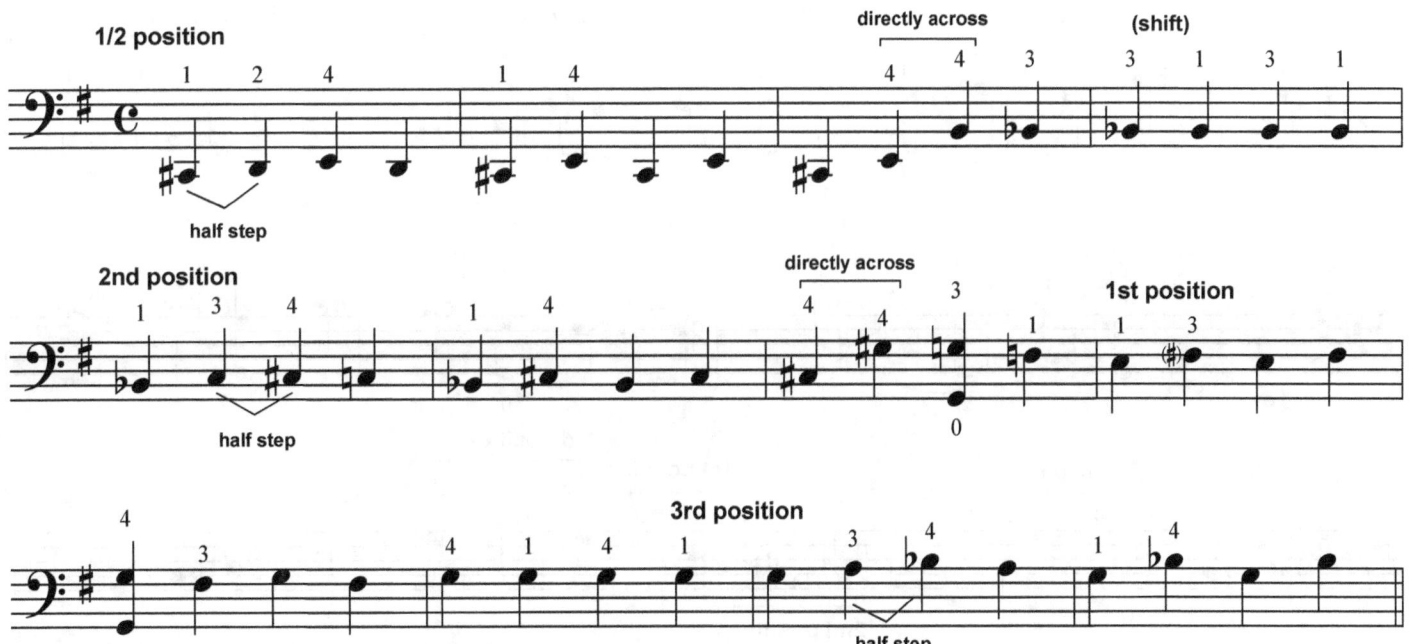

Definitions
Allegro.: brisk, lively
energico: play viorously, with energy

a piacere: at the pleasure or discretion of the performer
meno f: play less loudly

a tempo: resume the normal speed

Learning the Notes I: Measures 31-32

©2020 C. Harvey Publications All Rights Reserved.

Fluency
Measures 31-33

Learning the Notes
Measures 34-35

The Goltermann Concerto No. 4 Study Book for Cello

Left-Hand Rhythm: Measure 34

Fluency: Measures 34-35

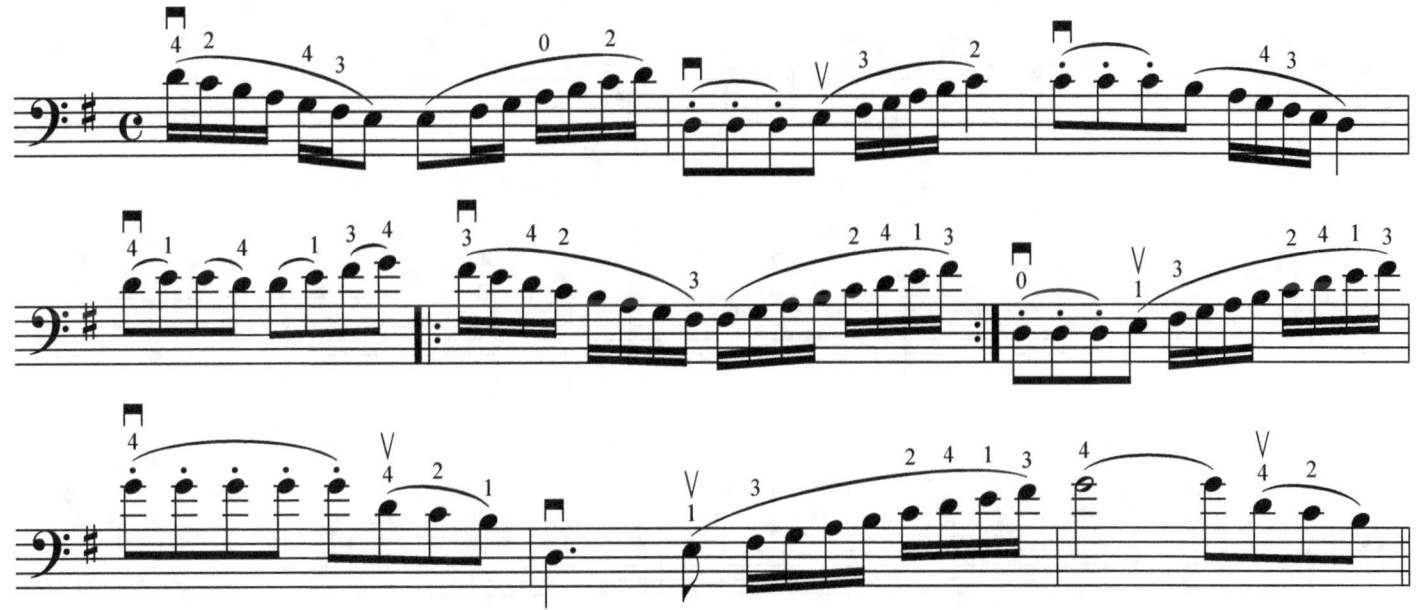

Bowing: Measures 34-35

©2020 C. Harvey Publications All Rights Reserved.

Third Position
Measures 35-37

Shifting Backwards
Measure 37

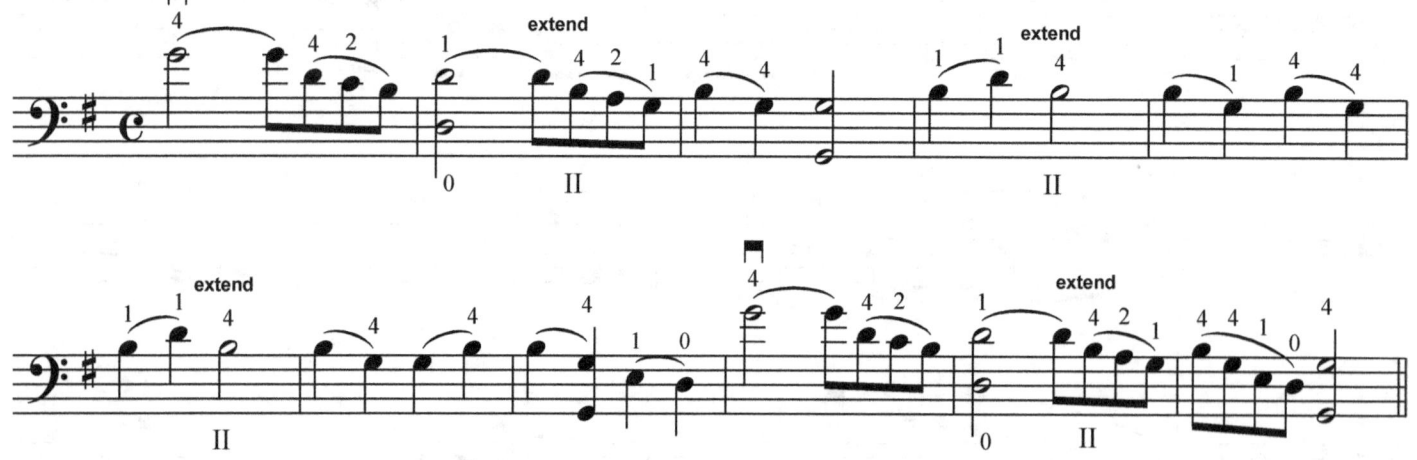

Learning the Notes
Measure 37

Learning the Rhythm
Measure 37

Working on Fluent Shifting
Measures 37-38

Long Slurs and Shifting
Measures 37-38

Grace Notes
Measures 37-38

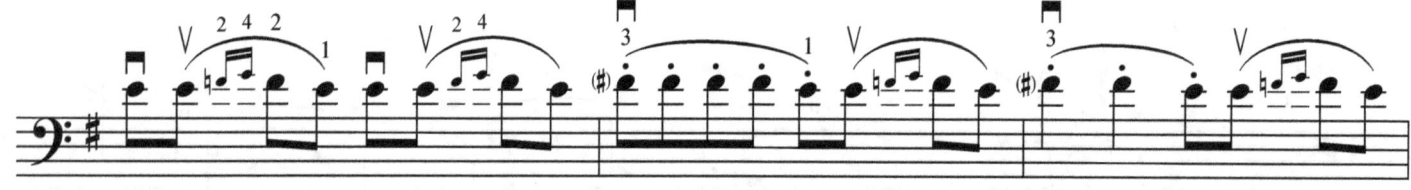
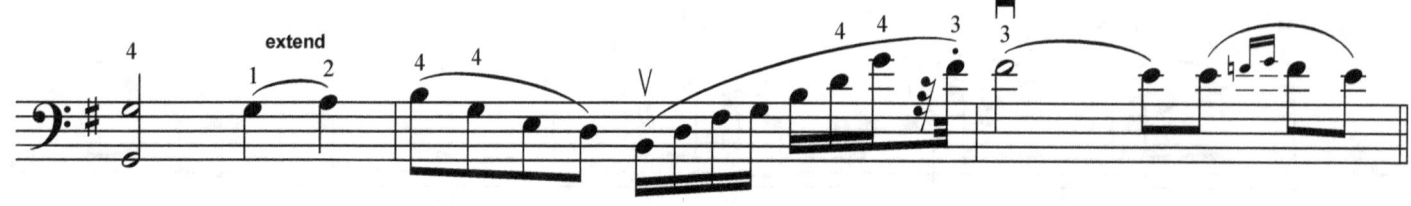

©2020 C. Harvey Publications   All Rights Reserved.

The Goltermann Concerto No. 4 Study Book for Cello

Shifting: Measures 38-39

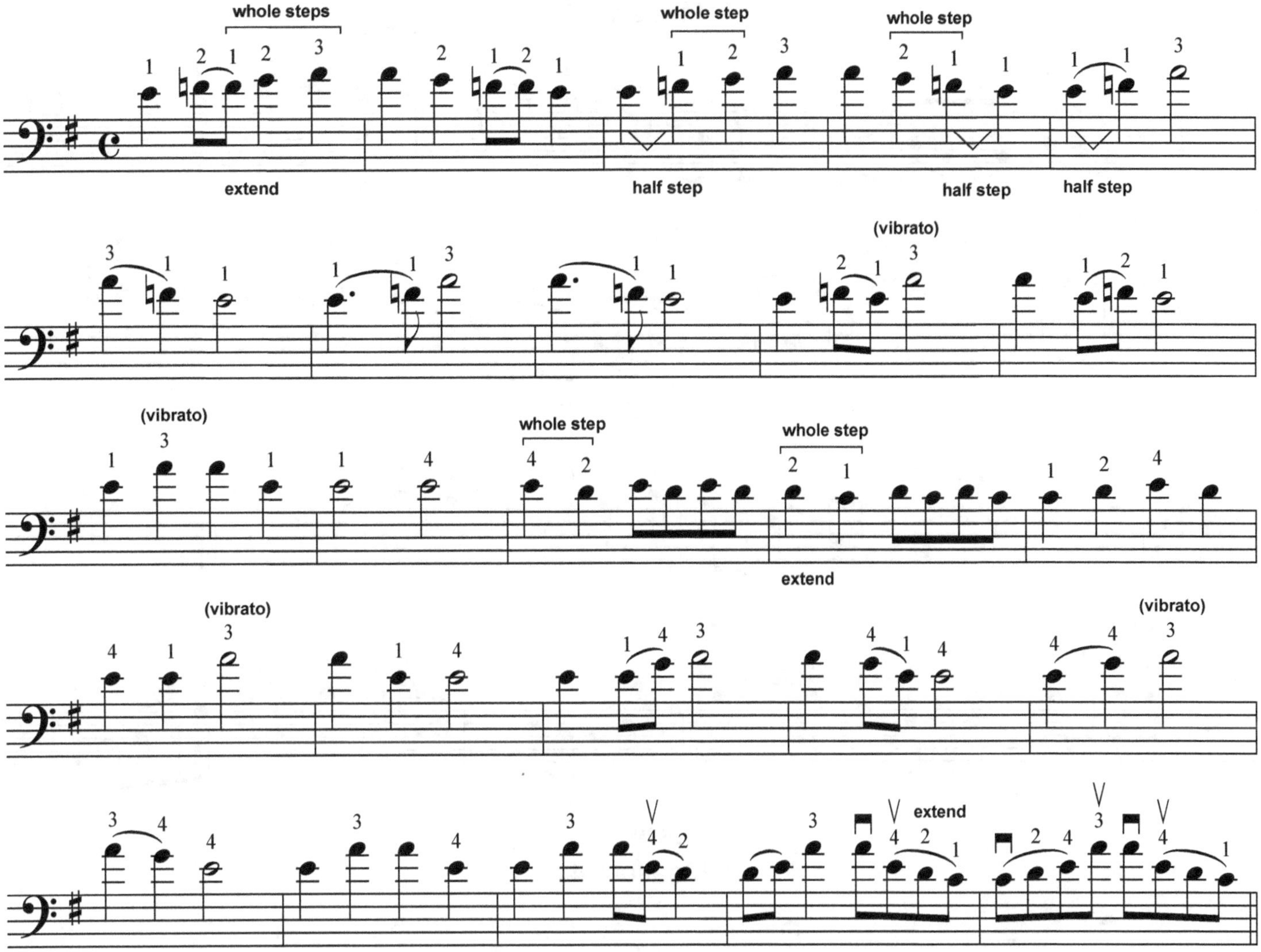

Rhythm: Measures 38-40

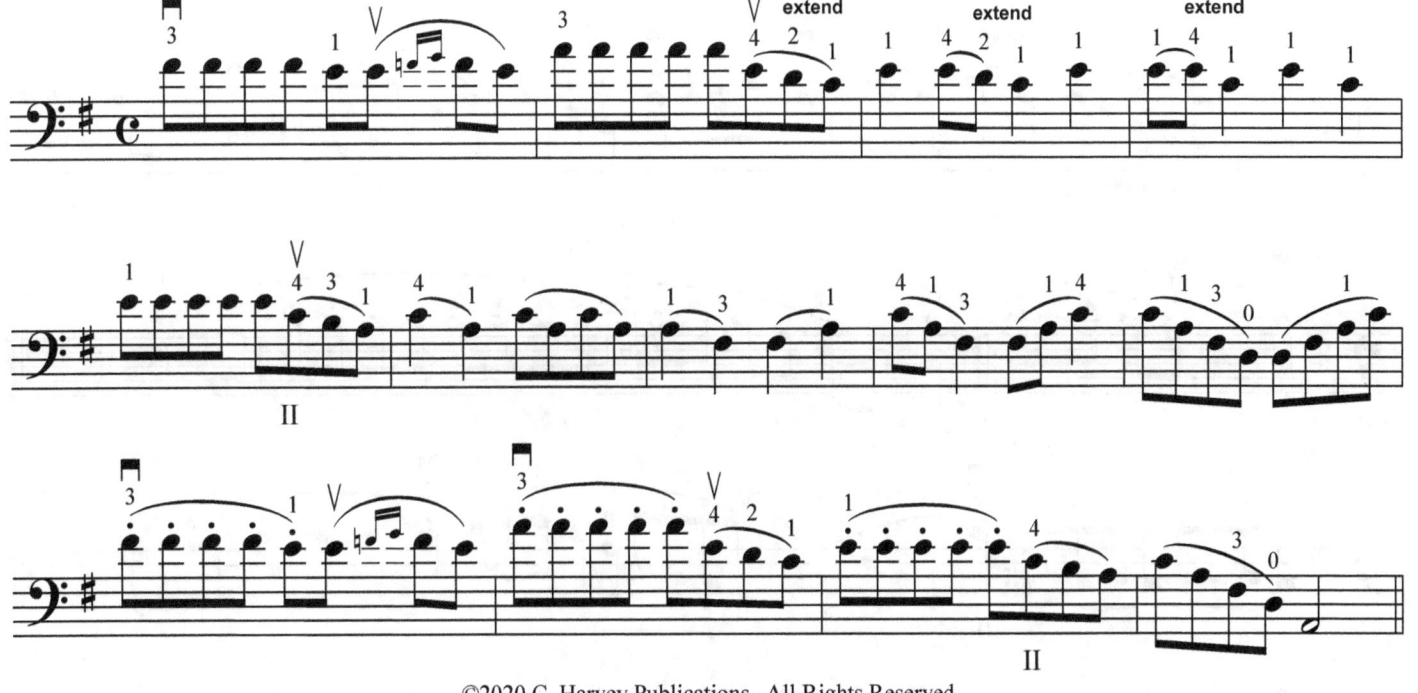

©2020 C. Harvey Publications All Rights Reserved.

Fluency I: Measure 41

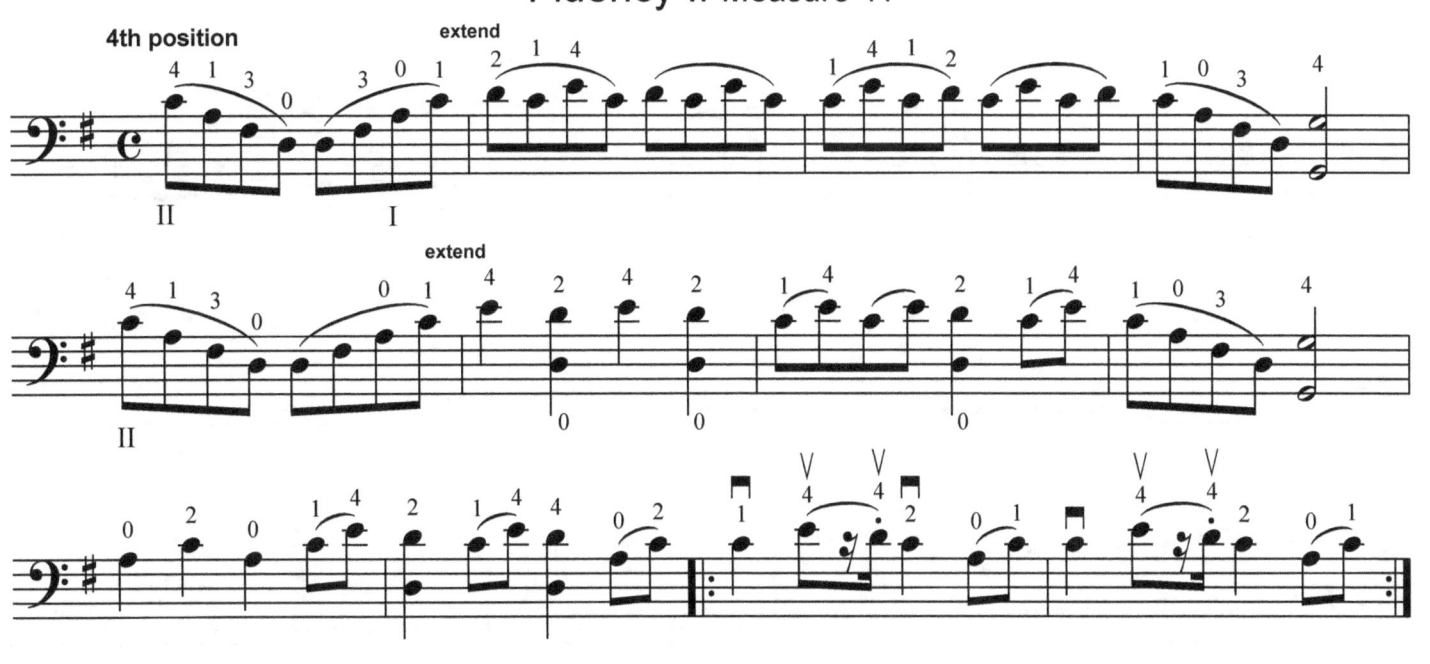

Fluency II: Measure 41

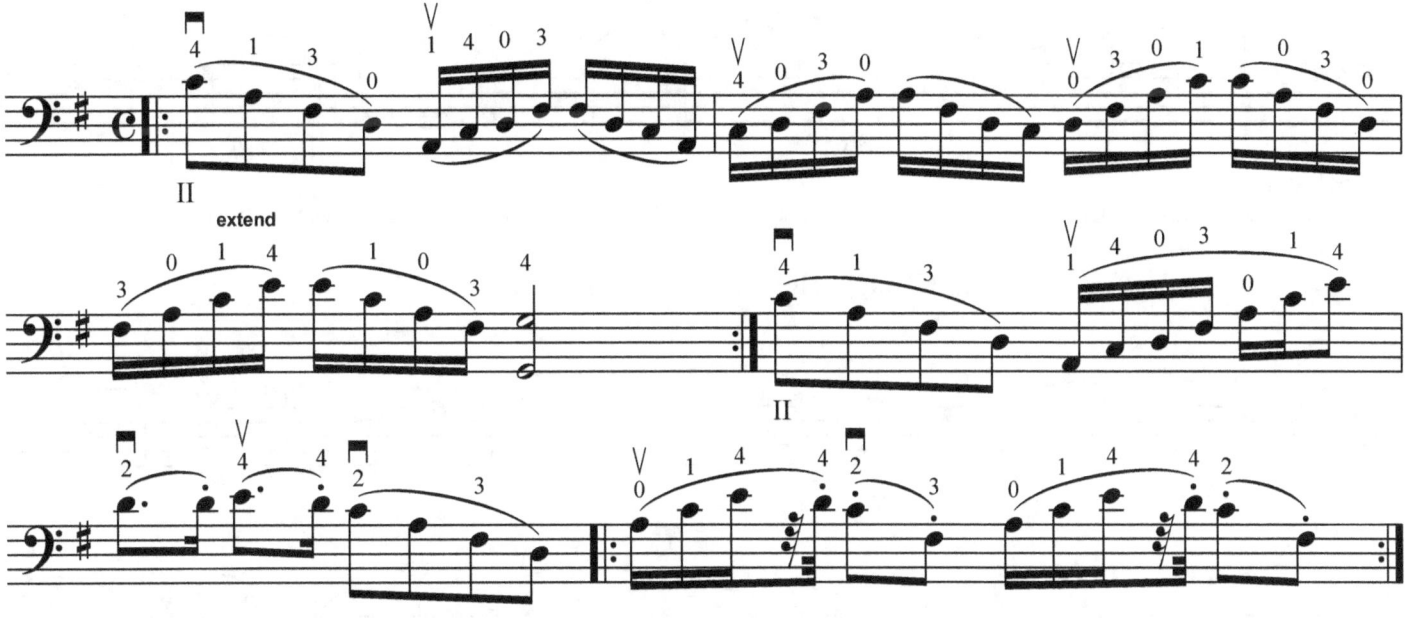

Shifting and Rhythm: Measure 42

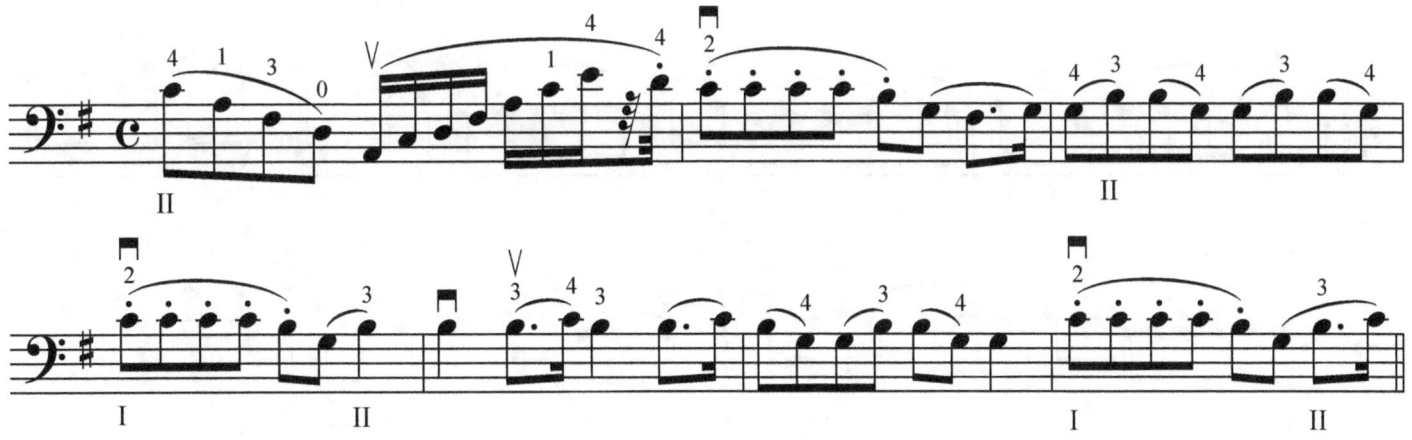

©2020 C. Harvey Publications   All Rights Reserved.

Concerto, First Movement: Section Two, Measures 43-56

Definitions
meno f: play less loudly   *dolce*: sweetly   *cresc.*: gradually increase the volume   *rall.*: a gradual slowing of the tempo

Learning the Notes: Measures 42-44

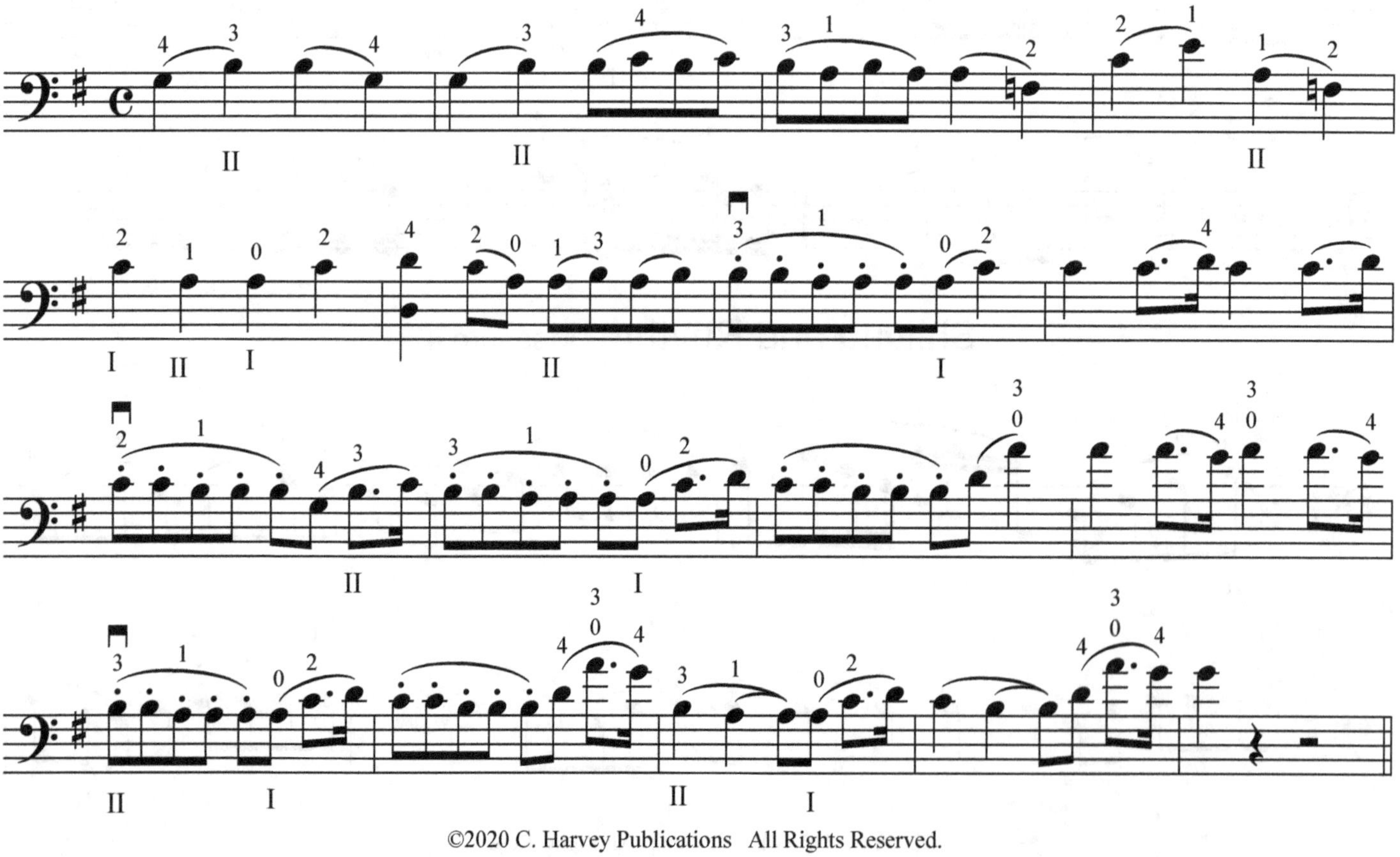

©2020 C. Harvey Publications All Rights Reserved.

Shifting
Measure 45

Learning the Notes
Measures 46-48

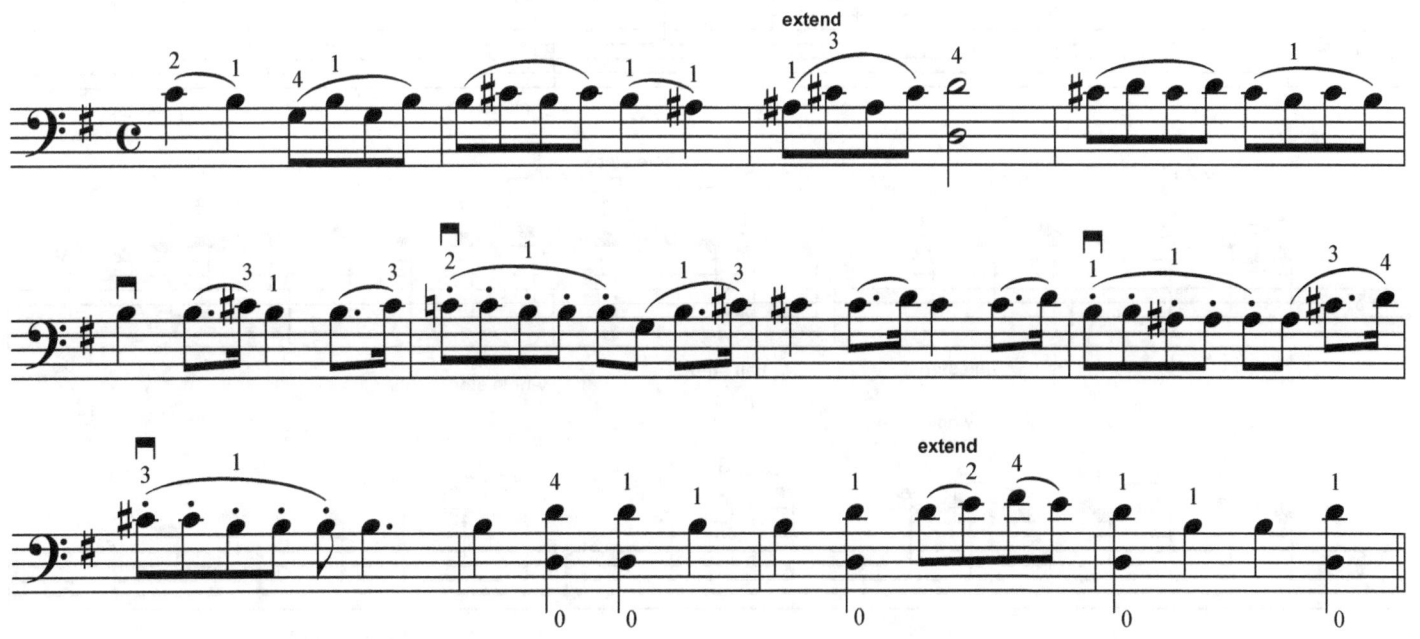

©2020 C. Harvey Publications All Rights Reserved.

Shifting I
Measure 48

Shifting II
Measure 48

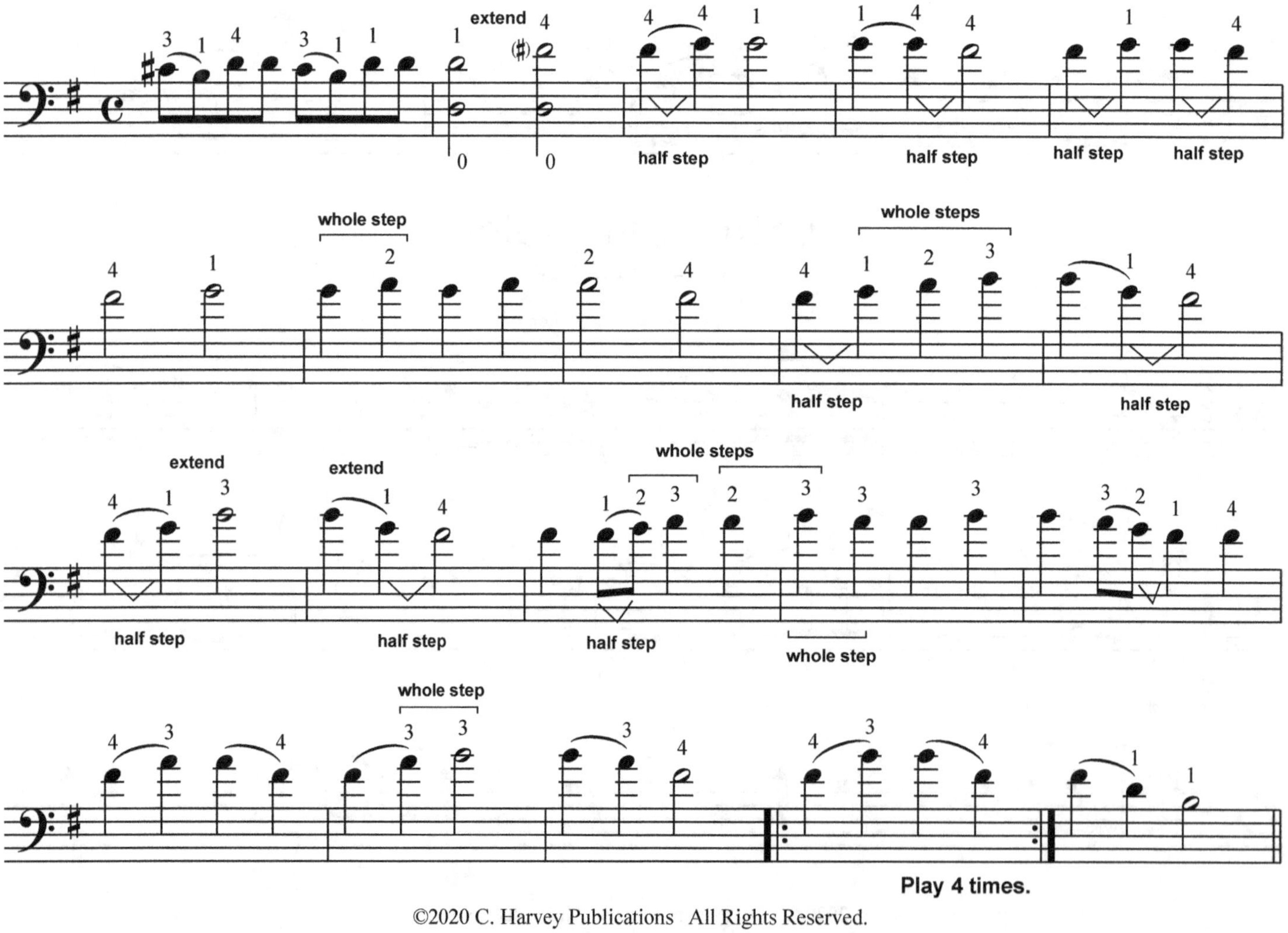

Play 4 times.

The Goltermann Concerto No. 4 Study Book for Cello

Shifting III: Measures 48-49

Shifting IV: Measures 48-49

©2020 C. Harvey Publications All Rights Reserved.

The Goltermann Concerto No. 4 Study Book for Cello 21

Rhythm
Measures 52-57

Don't articulate the eighth notes inside the slurs in this duet; tie them together. They are written this way to help you count in eighth notes for this section.

Rhythm Duet
Measures 52-57

©2020 C. Harvey Publications All Rights Reserved.

Definition
a tempo: resume the normal speed

Concerto, First Movement
Section Three: Measures 57-62

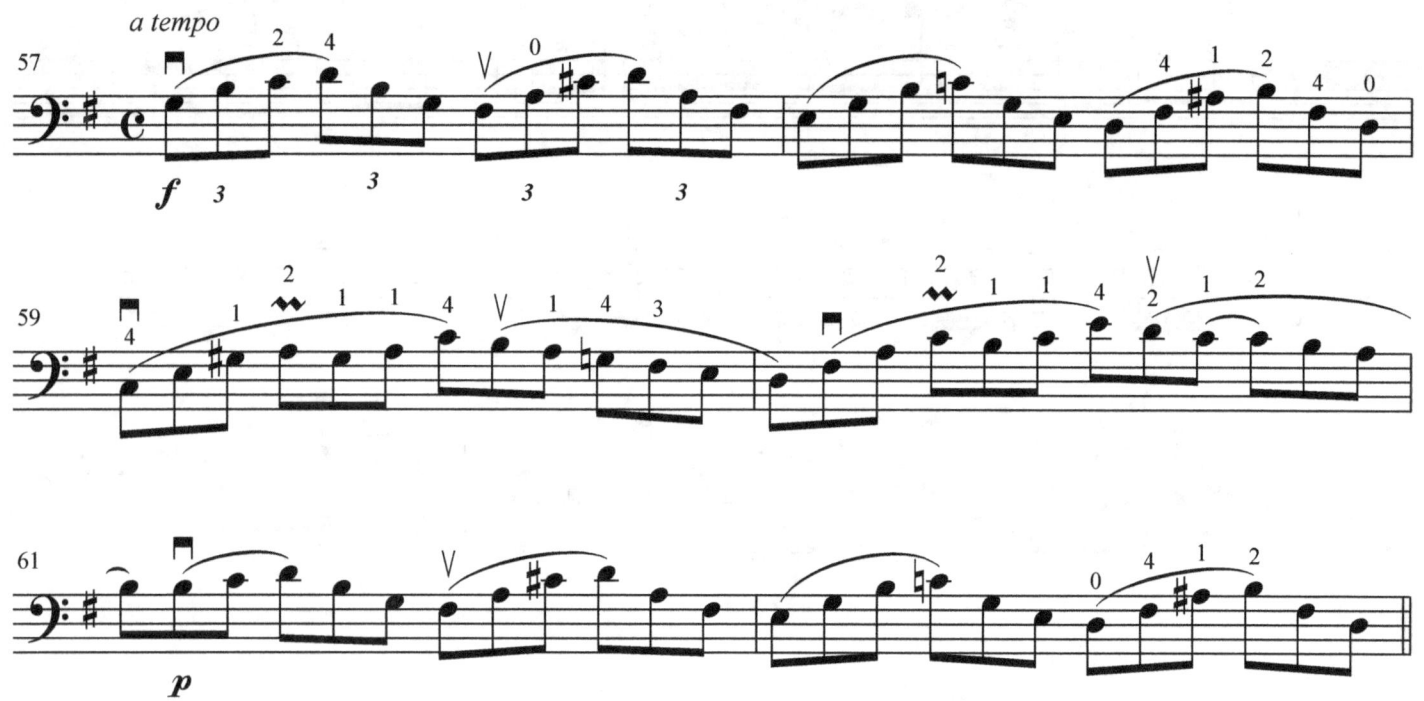

Finger Exercise and String Crossing: Measures 57-58

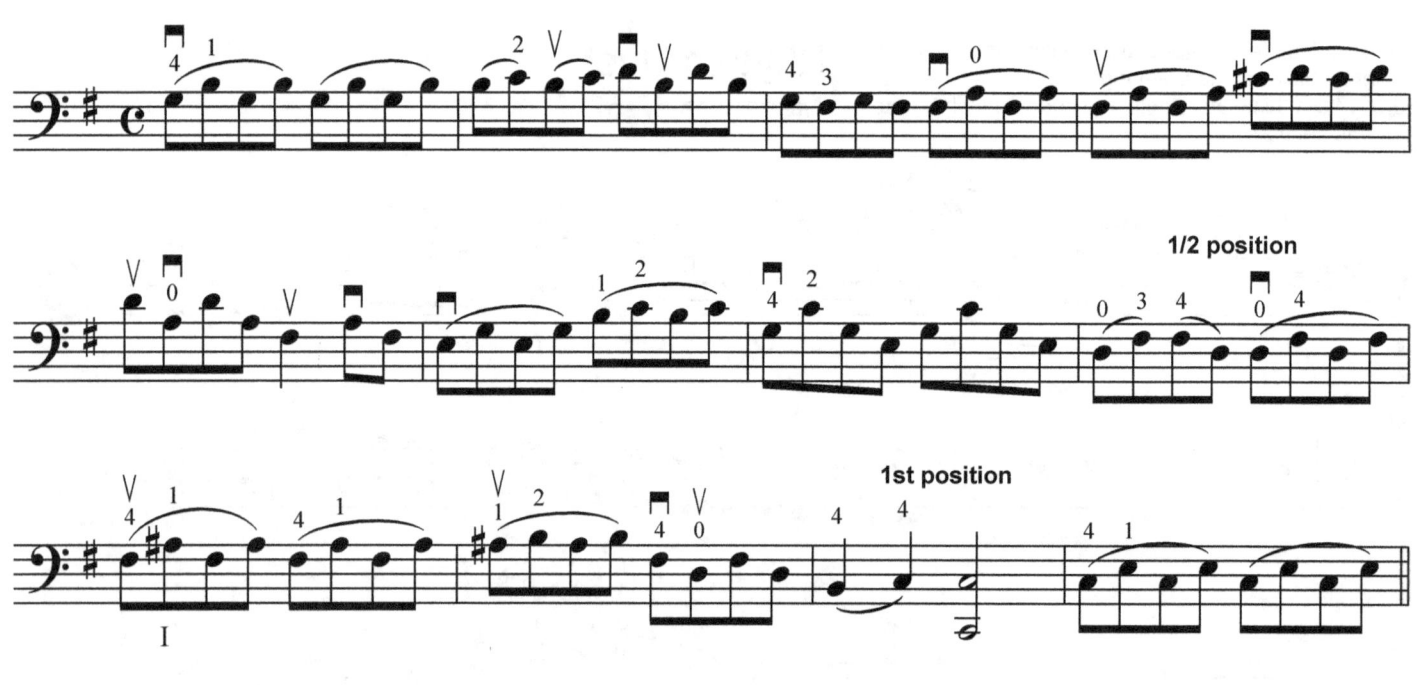

Bowing: Measures 57-58

©2020 C. Harvey Publications All Rights Reserved.

Finger Exercise Challenge: Measures 57-58

Learning the Notes I: Measure 59

Learning the Notes II: Measure 59

Learning the Notes III: Measure 60

Shifting Intensive
Measures 59-60

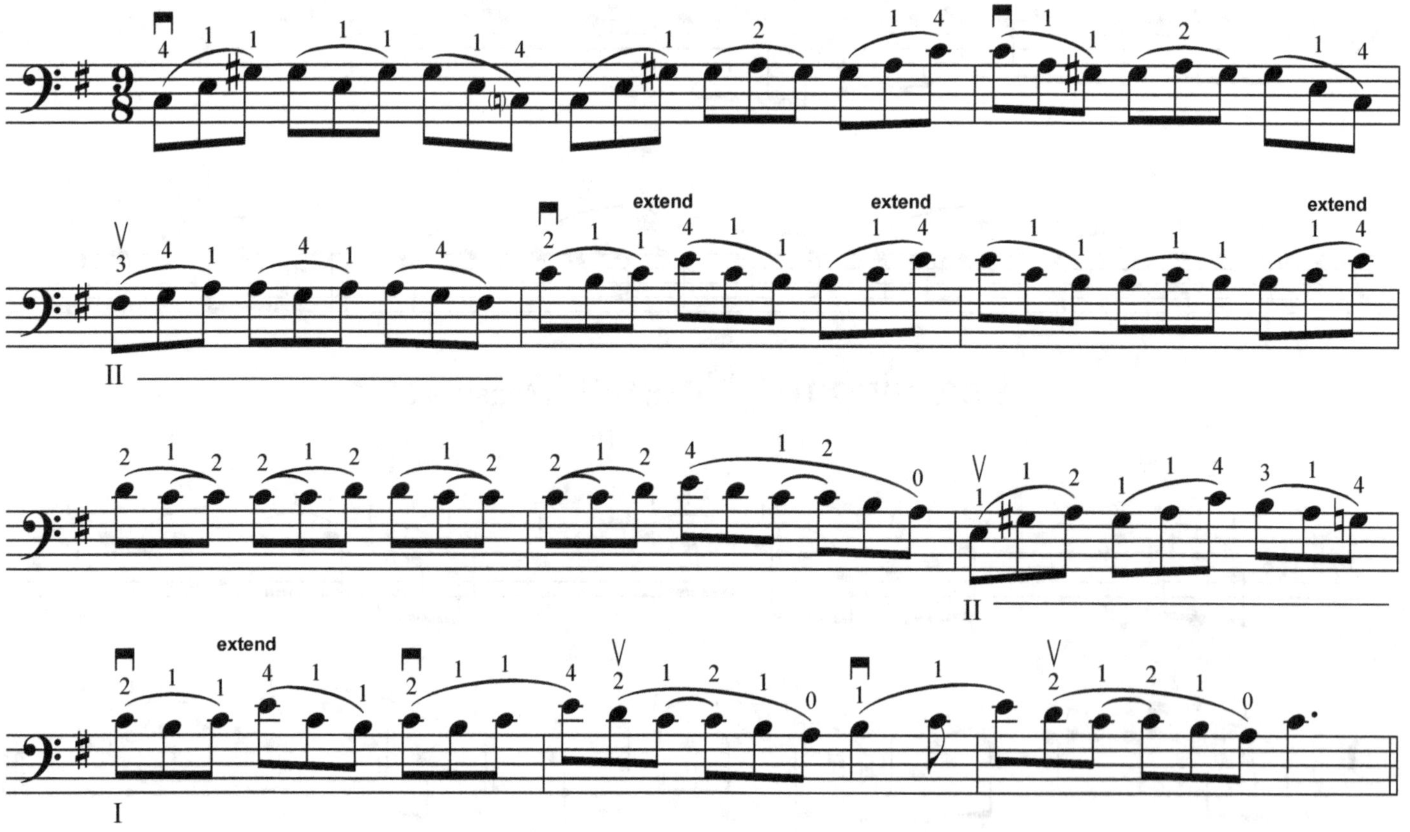

Mordents
Measures 59-72

Incorporating the Mordants
Measures 59-60

Concerto, First Movement
Section Four: Measures 63-77

Definitions
dolce: sweetly
cresc.: gradually increase the volume

Learning the Notes
Measure 63

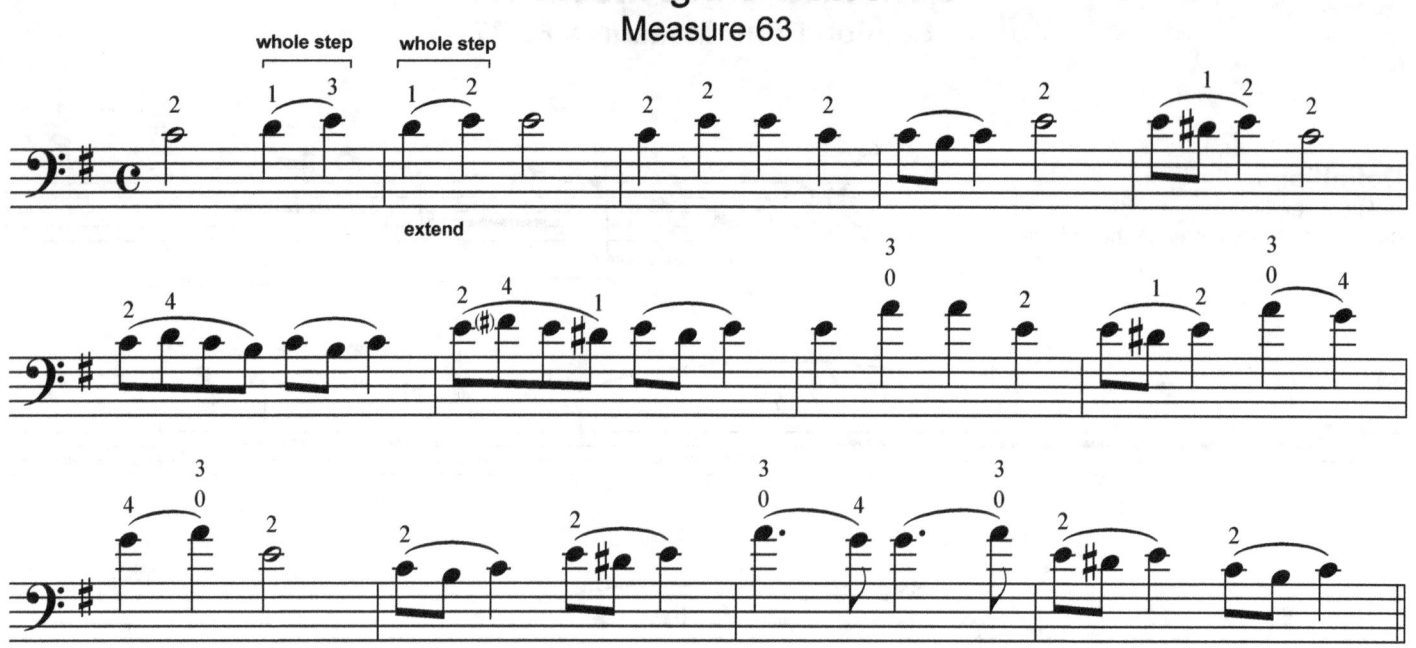

Mordants and Shifting
Measures 63-64

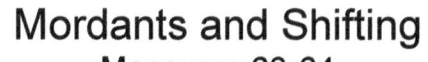

The Goltermann Concerto No. 4 Study Book for Cello

Shifting I
Measures 64-66

Shifting II
Measures 66-68

Bowing Fragments I
Measures 65-68

extend

Bowing Fragments II
Measures 65-68

Repeat each section several times, playing faster each time.

Bowing Fragments III
Measures 65-68

Repeat each section several times, playing faster each time.

Bowing and Shifting I
Measures 65-68

©2020 C. Harvey Publications All Rights Reserved.

Bowing and Shifting II: Measures 65-68

Fluency: Measures 65-68

Shifting and Mordents
Measures 69-70

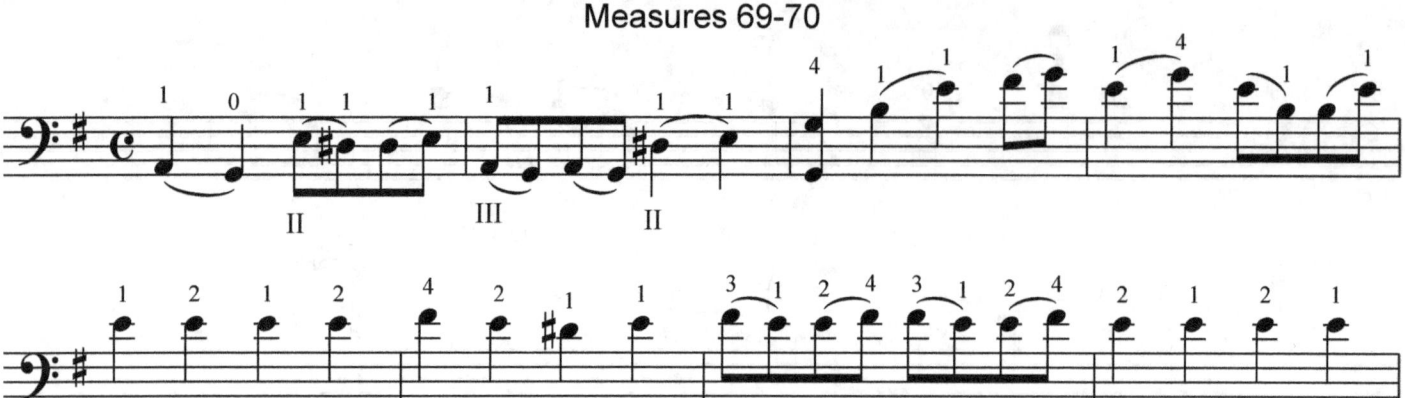

Learning the Notes
Measures 70-71

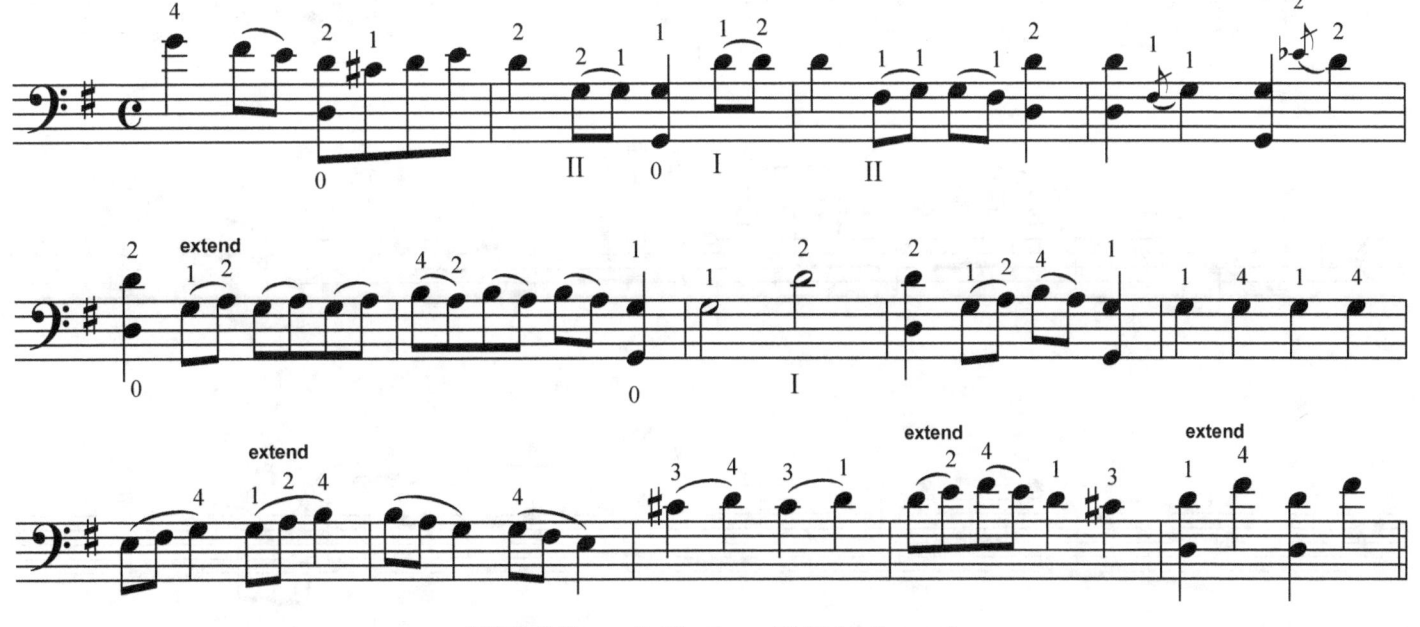

Shifting III

Measures 73-77

Play 4 times.

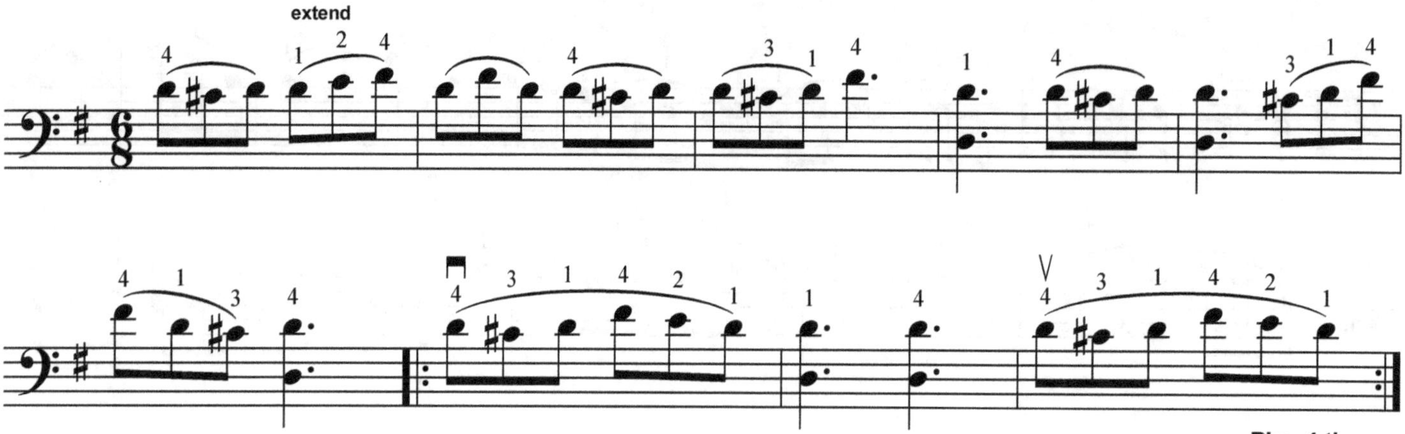

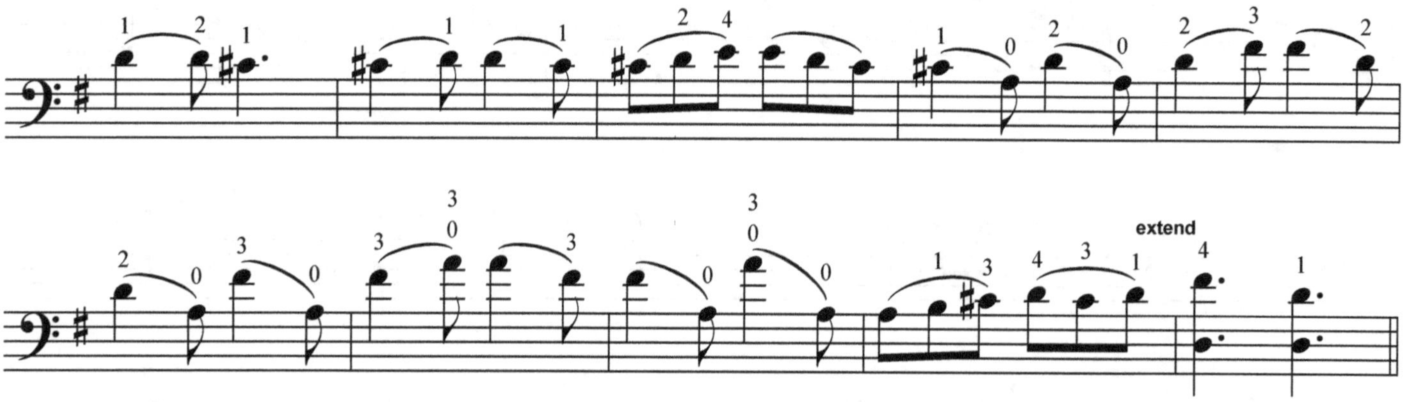

Learning the Bowing with Staccato

Measures 69-71

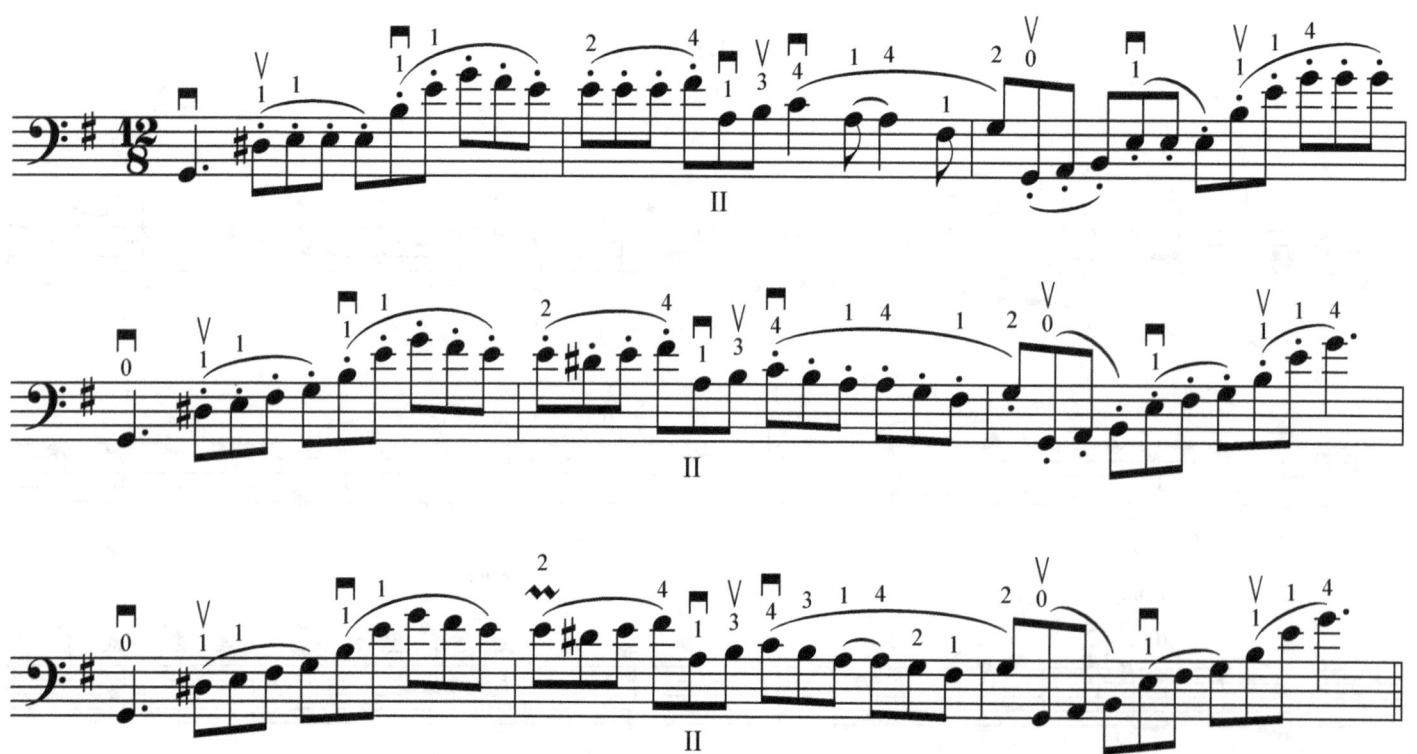

The Goltermann Concerto No. 4 Study Book for Cello 37

General Bowing Agility Study

Bowing Fragments
Measures 70-74

Play each repeated section 4 times.

©2020 C. Harvey Publications All Rights Reserved.

Bowing Fluency I: Measures 72-75

Bowing Fluency II: Measures 74-77

The Goltermann Concerto No. 4 Study Book for Cello

Concerto, First Movement
Section Five: Measures 79-97a

Poco meno mosso

mf *a piacere* *rallent.* *p* *con affetto*

mf

cresc. *rallent.* *p* *a tempo*

mf *string. e cresc.*

rallent.

Definitions
a piacere: at the pleasure or discretion of the performer   *rallent.*: a gradual slowing of the tempo   *con affetto*: with affect, or emotion
Poco meno mosso: a little less quickly   *cresc.*: gradually increase the volume   *a tempo*: resume the normal speed
string. e cresc.: accelerate the tempo and increase the volume

Learning the Notes: Measure 79

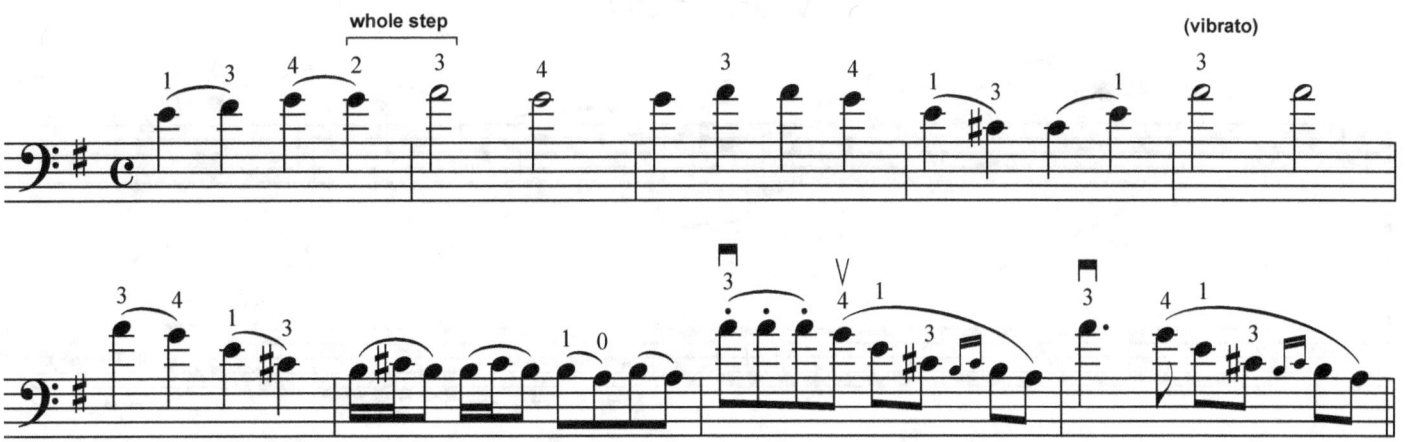

©2020 C. Harvey Publications All Rights Reserved.

Shifting and Rhythm
Measures 79-84

Learning the Notes
Measures 85-86

Notes and Rhythm I
Measures 86-87

Notes and Rhythm II
Measures 87-88

The Goltermann Concerto No. 4 Study Book for Cello

Shifting I
Measures 89-92

Shifting II
Measures 93-96

©2020 C. Harvey Publications All Rights Reserved.

Rhythm
Measures 85-96

Concerto, First Movement
Section Six: Measures 97-108

Definitions
con leggerezza: with lightness
meno f: play less loudly
rallent.: a gradual slowing of the tempo
cresc.: gradually increase the volume

Transition Between Sections
Measures 95-97

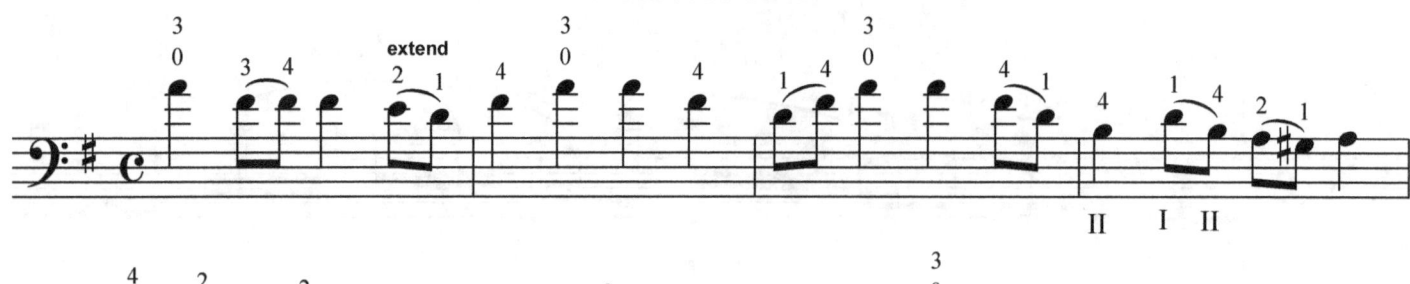

Finger Exercise I
Measures 97, 99

Repeat each section several times, playing faster each time.

Finger Exercise II
Measures 97, 99

Repeat each section several times, playing faster each time.

©2020 C. Harvey Publications All Rights Reserved.

The Goltermann Concerto No. 4 Study Book for Cello

Shifting Backwards
Measures 97, 99

Note: for the clearest sound and fastest shifting, shift backwards to a curved 3rd finger after the harmonic. Play on the very tip of the finger. After playing the harmonic, the finger may need some conscious work to re-curve and play the next note.

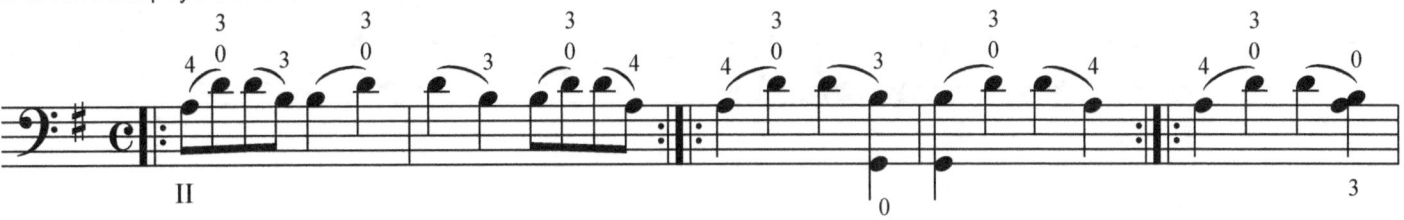

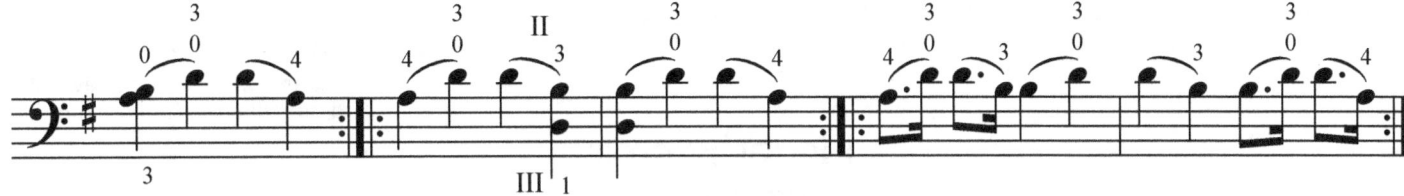

Speed Study
Measures 97, 99

Shift to and from a curved third finger.

Repeat each section several times, playing faster each time.

Agility
Measures 97, 99

Shift to and from a curved third finger.

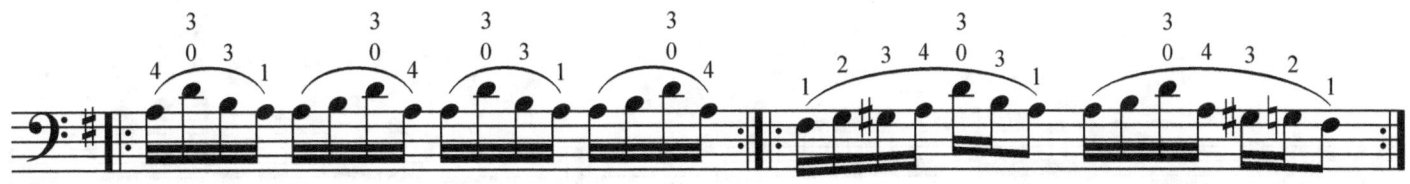

Repeat each section several times, playing faster each time.

©2020 C. Harvey Publications All Rights Reserved.

Shifting To and From the Harmonic
Measures 97, 99
Shift to and from a curved third finger.

Finger Exercise
Measures 97, 99

Repeat each section several times, playing faster each time.

The Goltermann Concerto No. 4 Study Book for Cello   49

Learning the Notes
Measure 98

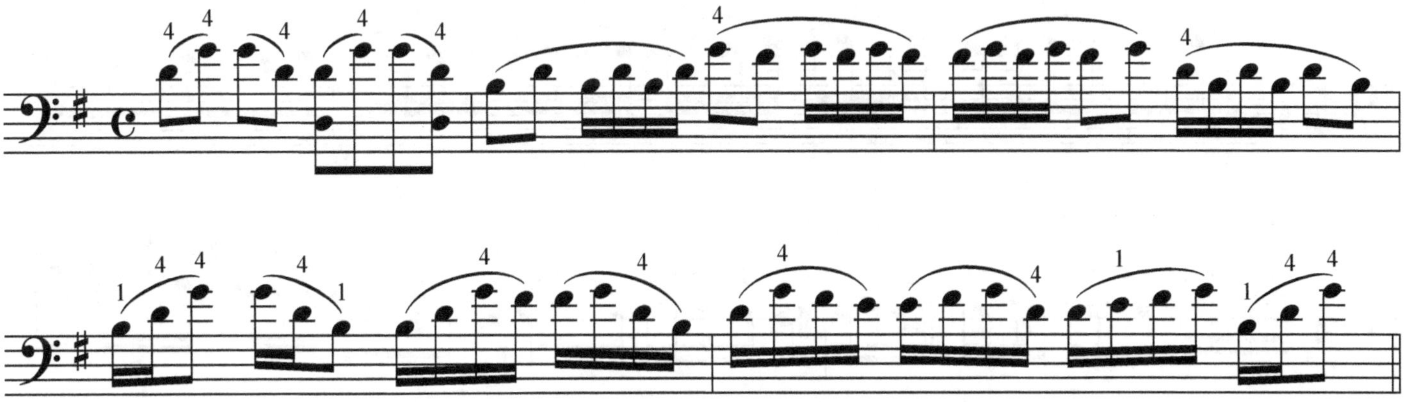

Shifting Back to Second Position
Measure 98

Bowing
Measure 98
Play these two measures in the upper 1/3 of the bow.

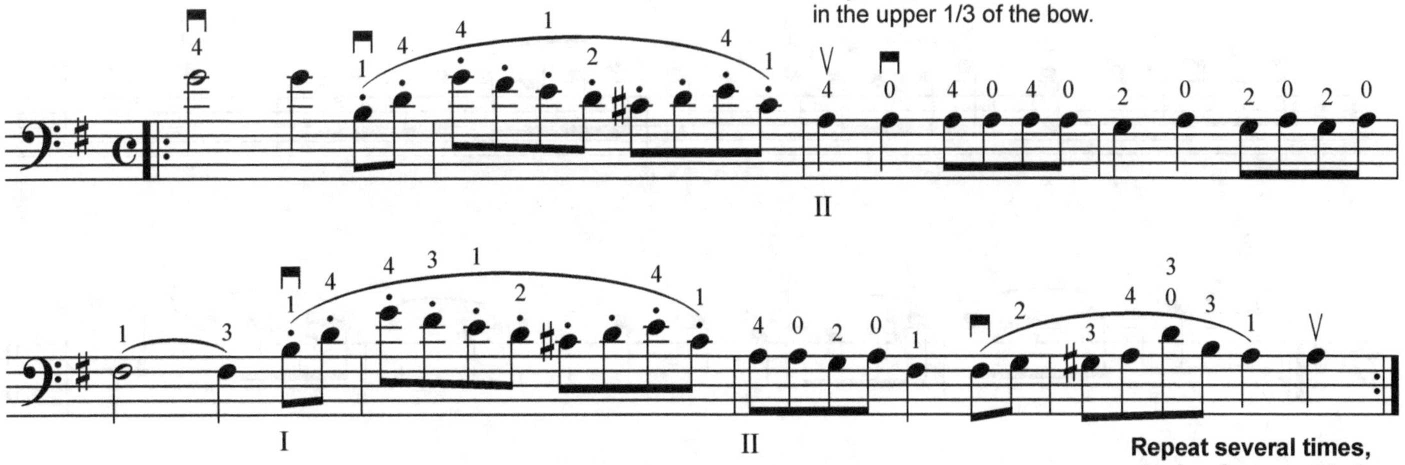

Repeat several times, playing faster each time.

©2020 C. Harvey Publications All Rights Reserved.

Agility
Measure 100

Learning the Notes
Measures 100-102

The Goltermann Concerto No. 4 Study Book for Cello   51

Shifting and Bowing
Measures 101-102

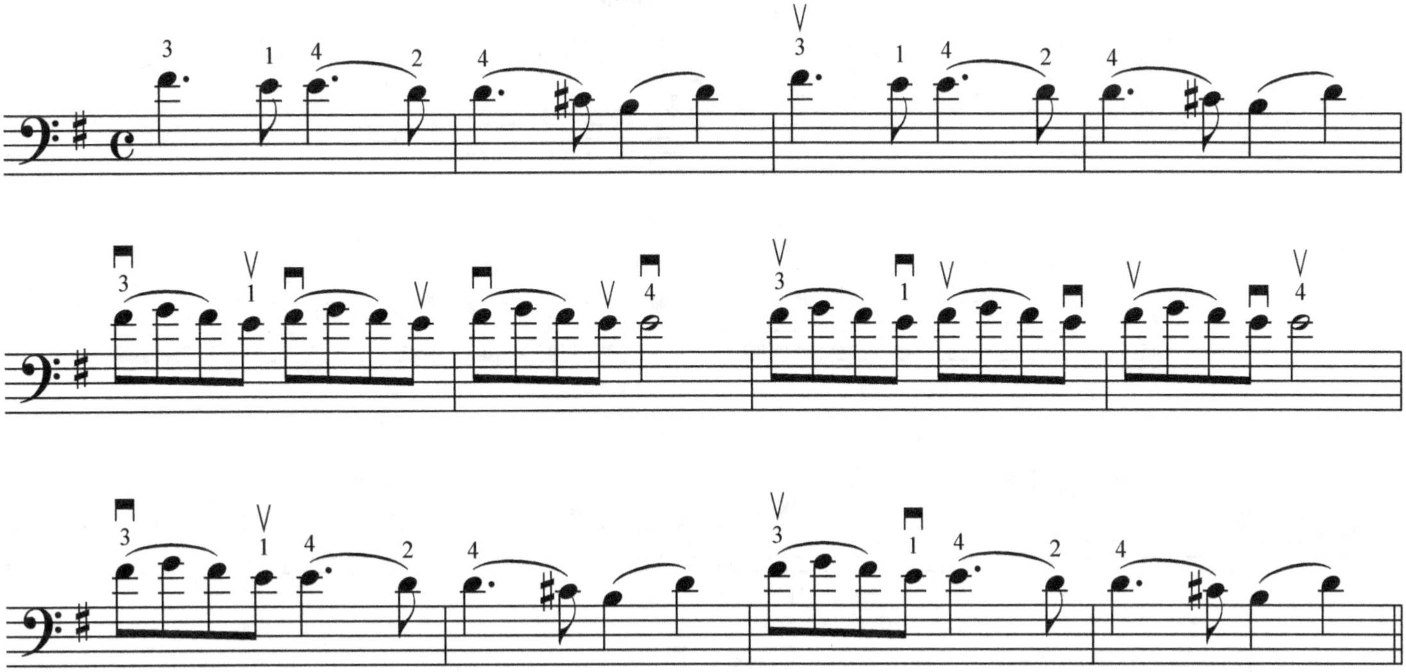

Shifting I
Measure 103

©2020 C. Harvey Publications   All Rights Reserved.

The Goltermann Concerto No. 4 Study Book for Cello

Third and Second Position: Measure 104

Shifting Backwards: Measure 104

©2020 C. Harvey Publications All Rights Reserved.

Bowing Fluency
Measures 103-105

On this page, repeat only if a section does not feel comfortable.

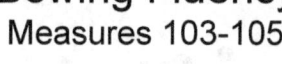

The Goltermann Concerto No. 4 Study Book for Cello

Shifting
Measure 105

Bowing
Measure 105

©2020 C. Harvey Publications All Rights Reserved.

Shifting I
Measures 105-106

Shifting II
Measure 106

The Goltermann Concerto No. 4 Study Book for Cello 57

©2020 C. Harvey Publications   All Rights Reserved.

The Goltermann Concerto No. 4 Study Book for Cello

Intonation: Measures 107-108

Agility and Speed: Measures 107-108

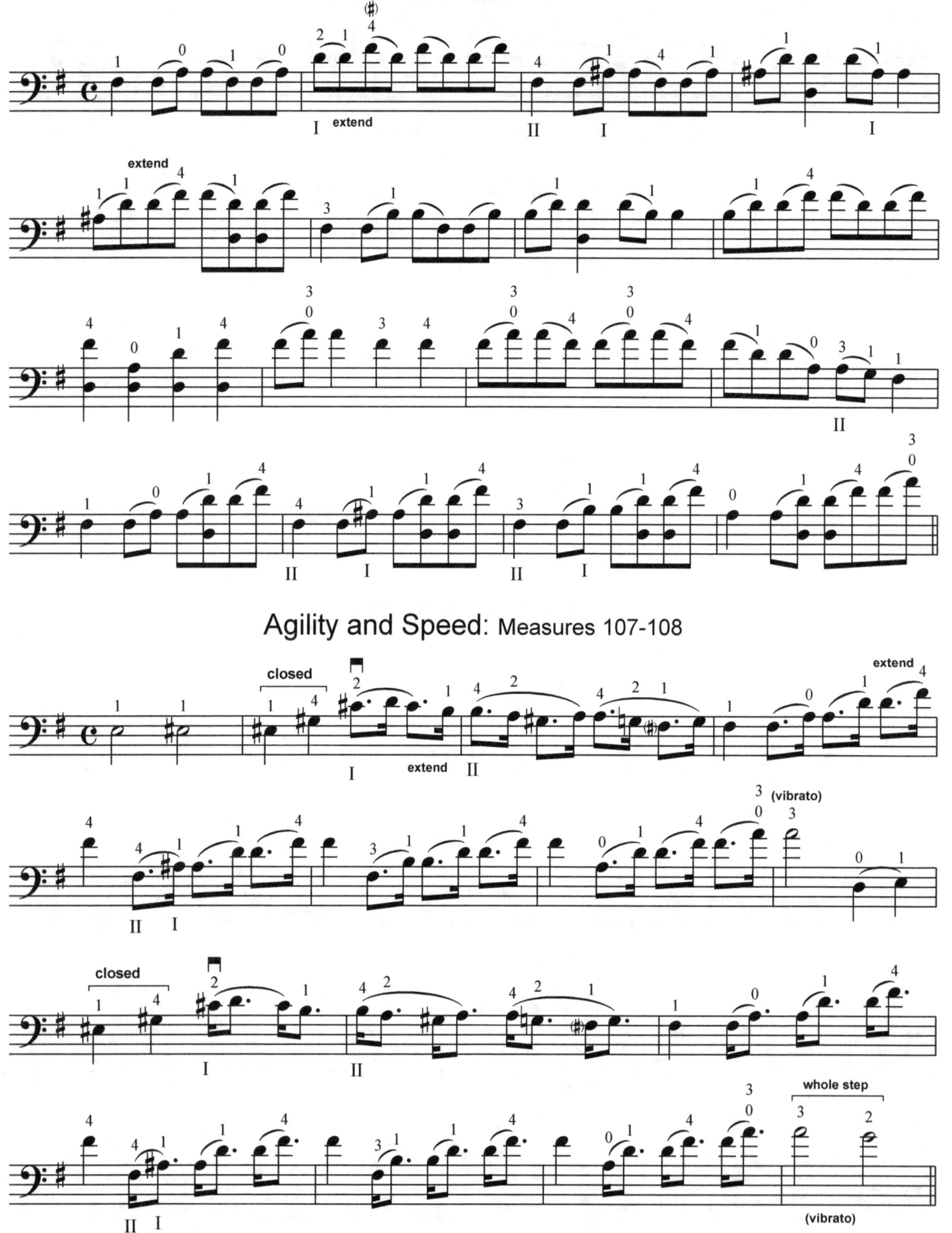

©2020 C. Harvey Publications   All Rights Reserved.

Concerto, First Movement
Section Seven: Measures 109-119 (end of movement)

Alternate ending

Definitions
fz : *forzando* or a forceful accent   *cresc.*: gradually increase the volume

The Goltermann Concerto No. 4 Study Book for Cello

String Crossing: Measure 111

Learning the Notes: Measures 111-112

Repeat several times, playing faster each time.

©2020 C. Harvey Publications All Rights Reserved.

Shifting
Measure 113

Shifting and String Crossing
Measure 113

The Goltermann Concerto No. 4 Study Book for Cello

Playing Harmonics

- A harmonic is an overtone that can be created by touching the string very lightly (not pressing the string down.)
- Play a harmonic with only one finger on the string and play on the tip of that finger.
- Be precise; harmonics are clearest if you are playing on the center of the note.
- The harmonics below are numbered just for this book; there are many other harmonics on the cello not listed on the chart.

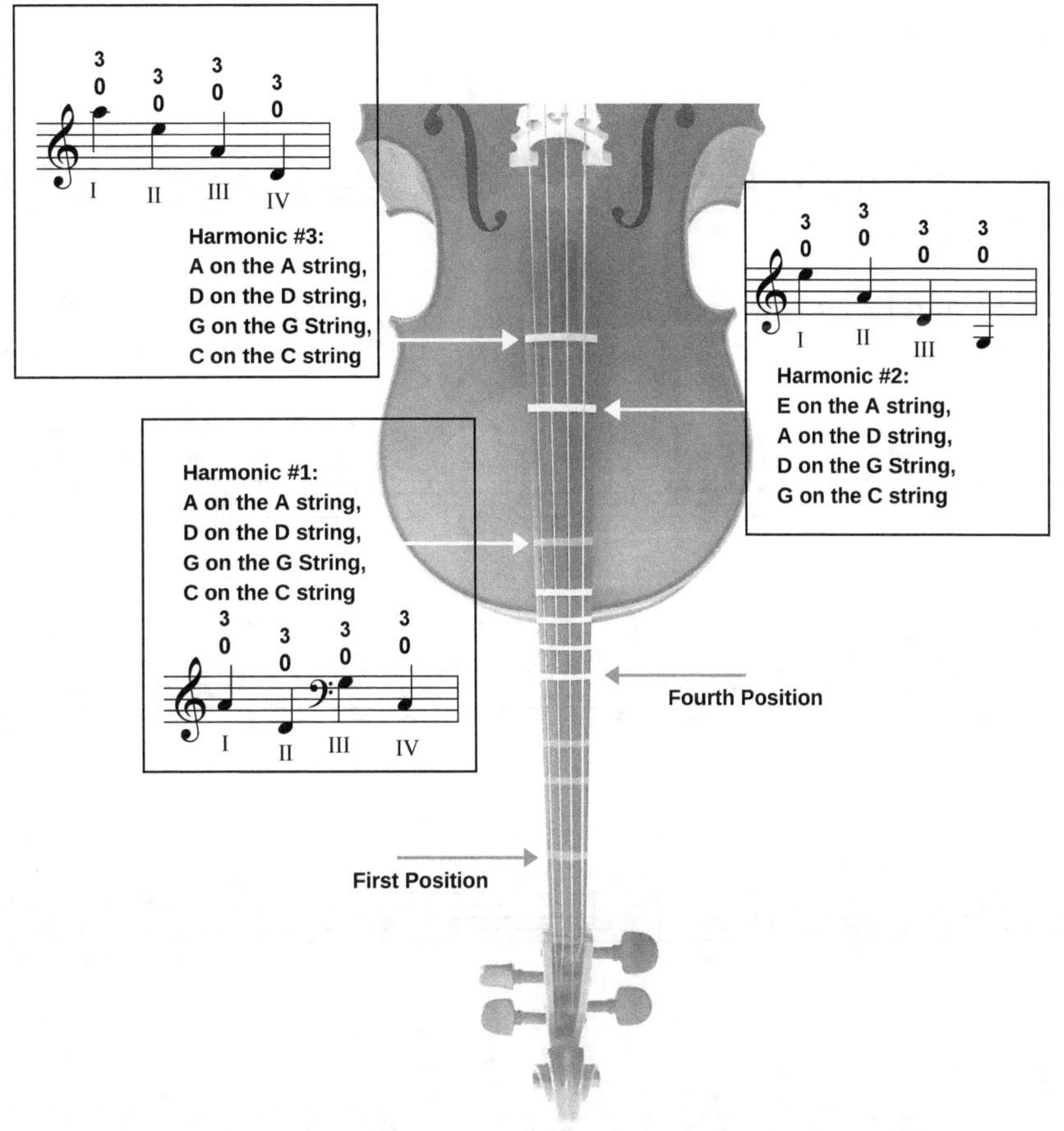

©2020 C. Harvey Publications All Rights Reserved.

Learning the Harmonics
Measure 114

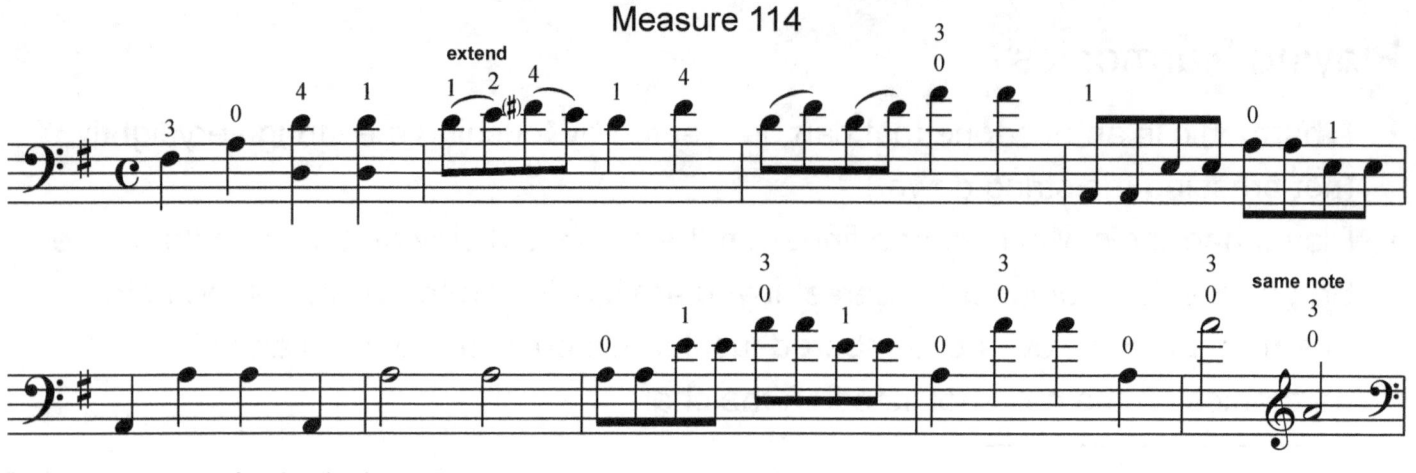

These harmonics can be found on the chart on page 65.

Shifting To and From Harmonics
Measure 114

Note: To shift between harmonics inside a slur, keep the bow moving on the string and lift your left hand up in the air as you shift; do not slide.

Finger Exercise
Measure 115

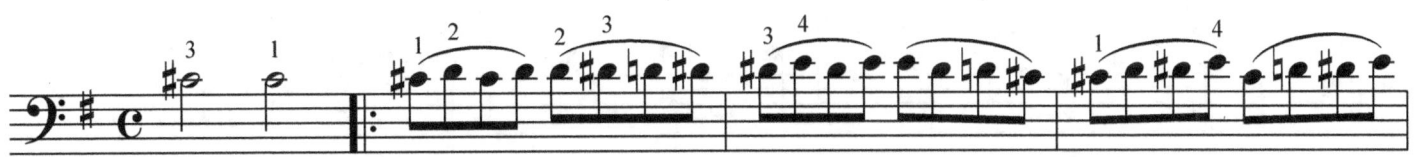

Shifting and Bowing
Measure 115

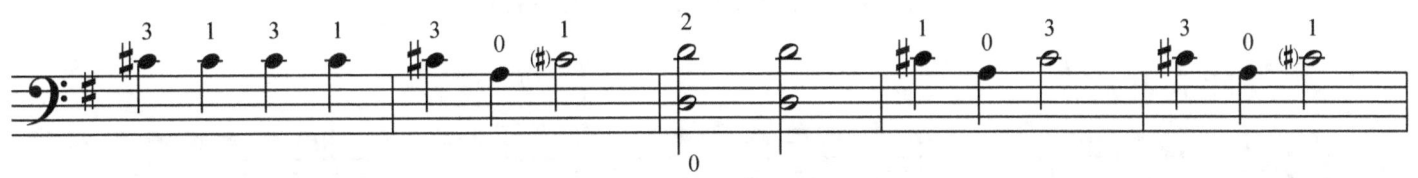
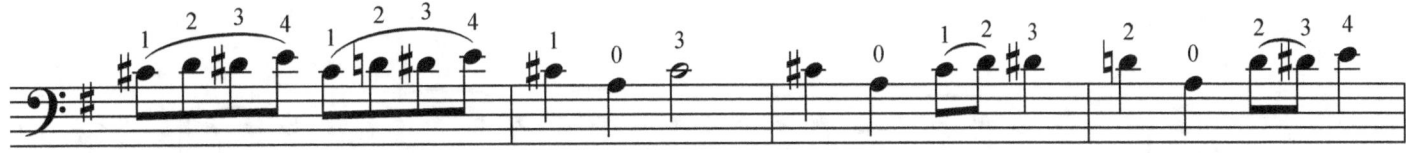

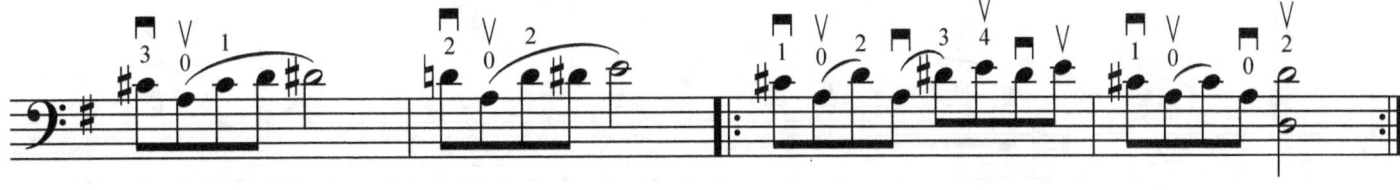

Shifting and Finger Agility: Measure 115

Note: These arrows are included to remind you to shift.

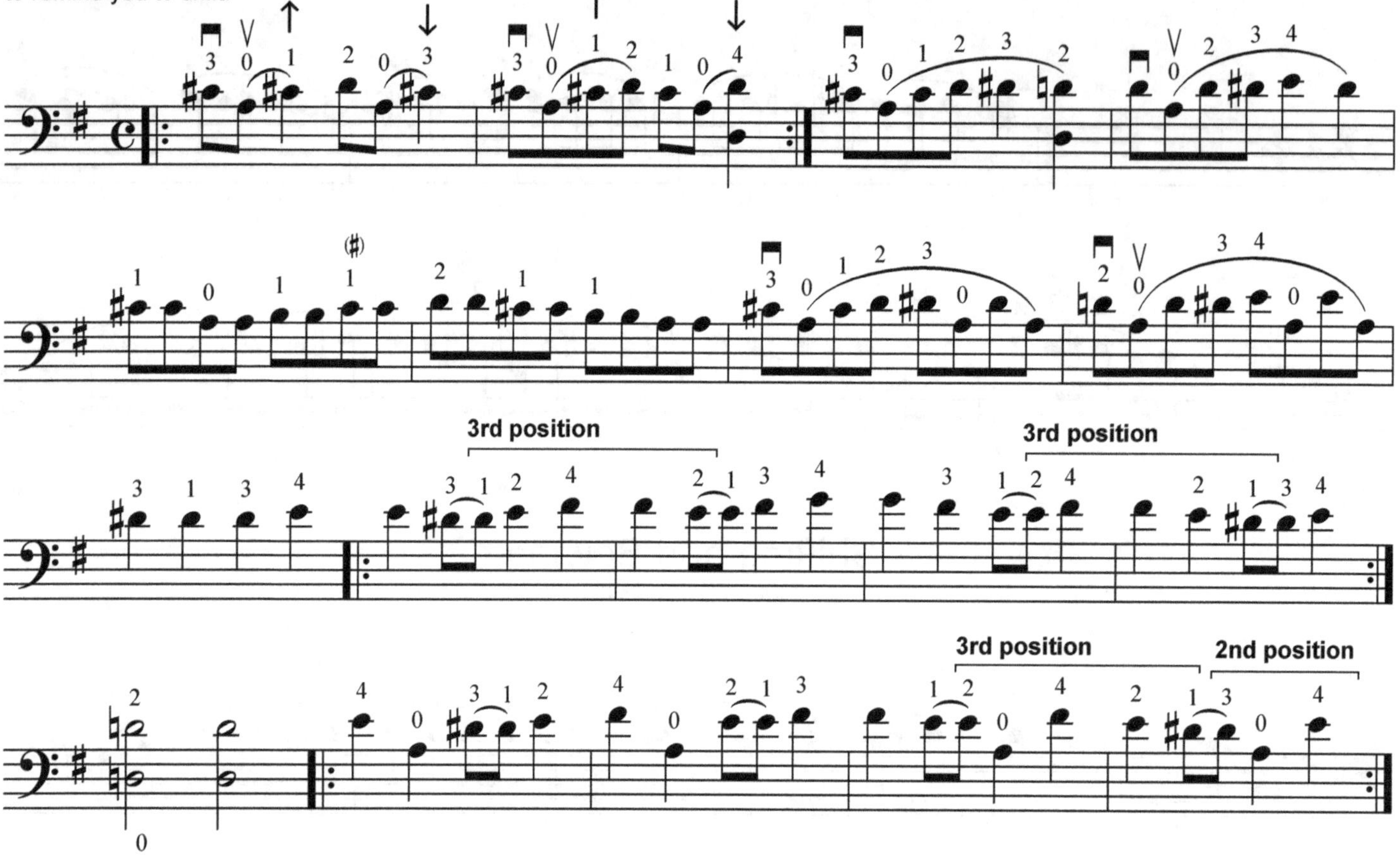

Learning the Positions: Measure 116

Shifting I
Measures 115-117

Shifting II
Measures 115-117

Fluent Shifting and Bowing
Measures 115-117

©2020 C. Harvey Publications All Rights Reserved.

Incorporating the Mordants: Measure 117

Staccato Bowing, Regular Fingering: Measures 118-119

The Goltermann Concerto No. 4 Study Book for Cello

Alternate Fingering: Exercise No. I
Measure 118b

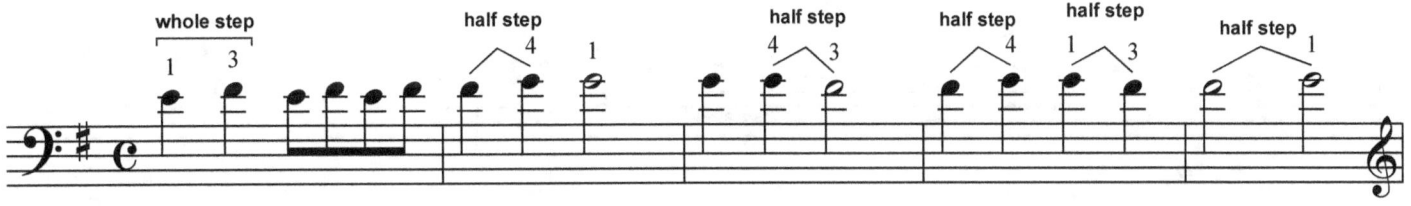

Alternate Fingering: Exercise No. II
Measure 118b

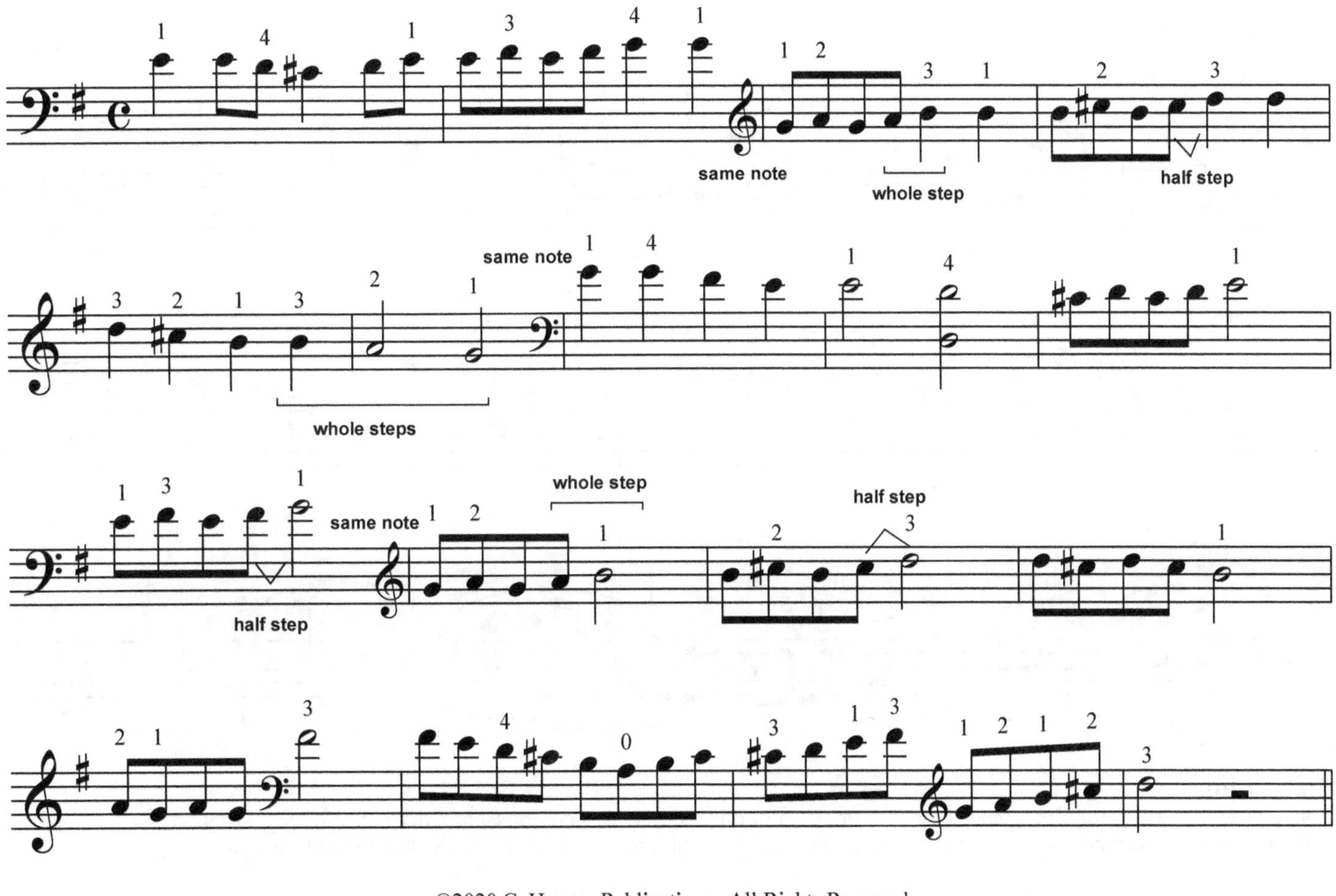

©2020 C. Harvey Publications All Rights Reserved.

Concerto, Second Movement
Section One: Measures 5-40

Definitions
Andantino: relaxed, moderato tempo, slightly faster than Andante
calmato: calmed, relaxed
cresc.: gradually increase the volume
con passione: dramatically, with emotion
dim.: gradually decrease the volume

©2020 C. Harvey Publications All Rights Reserved.

The Goltermann Concerto No. 4 Study Book for Cello

73

Learning the Shifting
Measures 5-13

Note: Play this exercise with vibrato
as soon as you have learned the notes.

Moving Through the Positions
Measures 5-13

©2020 C. Harvey Publications All Rights Reserved.

Grace Notes
Measures 5-9

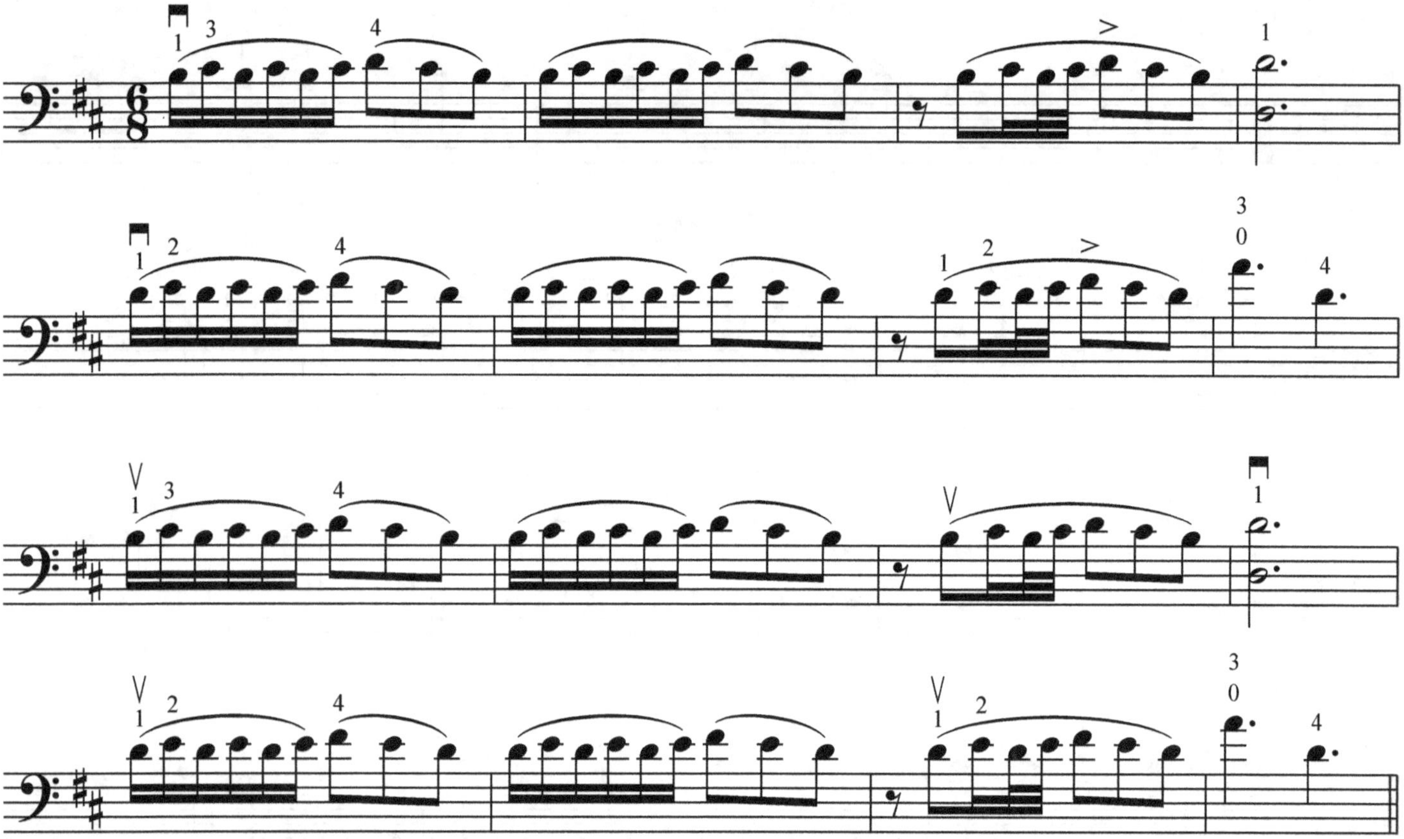

Rhythm
Measures 5-13

The Goltermann Concerto No. 4 Study Book for Cello 75

Shifting
Measures 13-15

Rhythm and Bowing
Measures 14-22

con passione

©2020 C. Harvey Publications All Rights Reserved.

Rhythm Duet
Measures 5-19

Shifting I
Measures 11-20

The Goltermann Concerto No. 4 Study Book for Cello   77

Shifting II
Measures 11-19

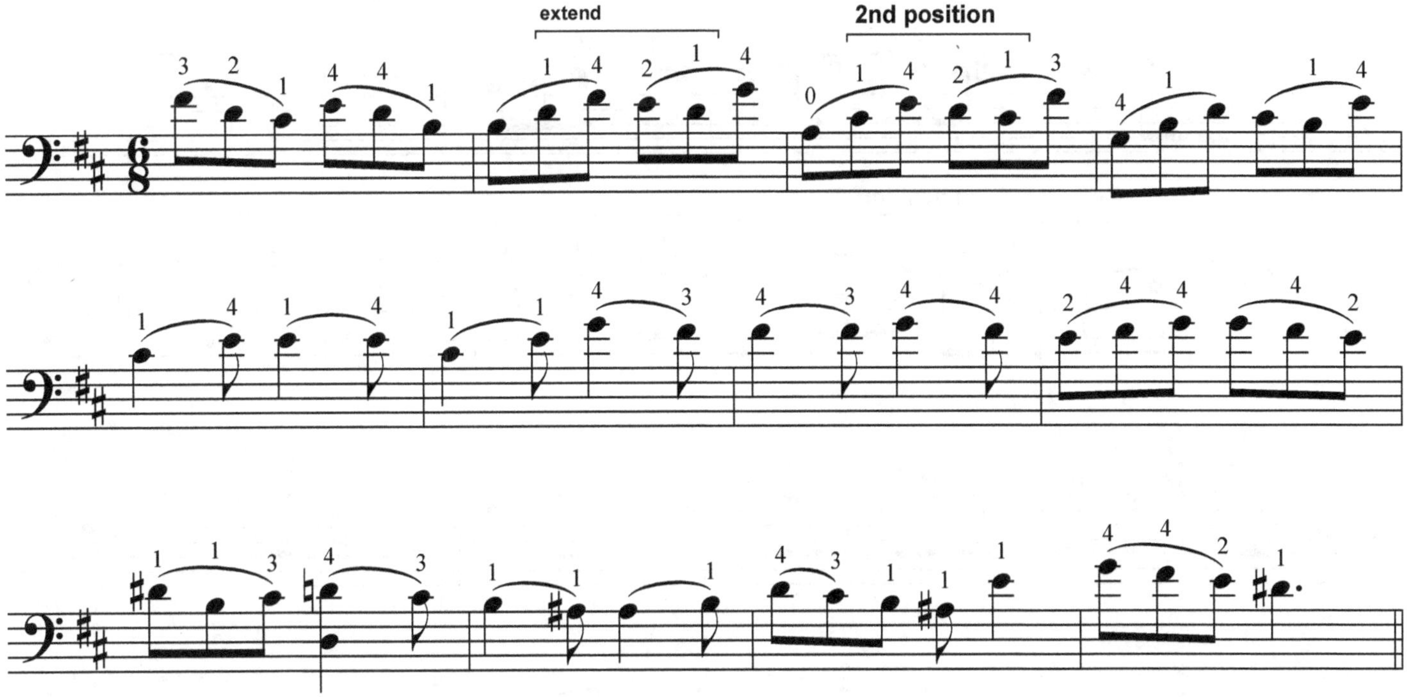

Position Study
Measures 19-31

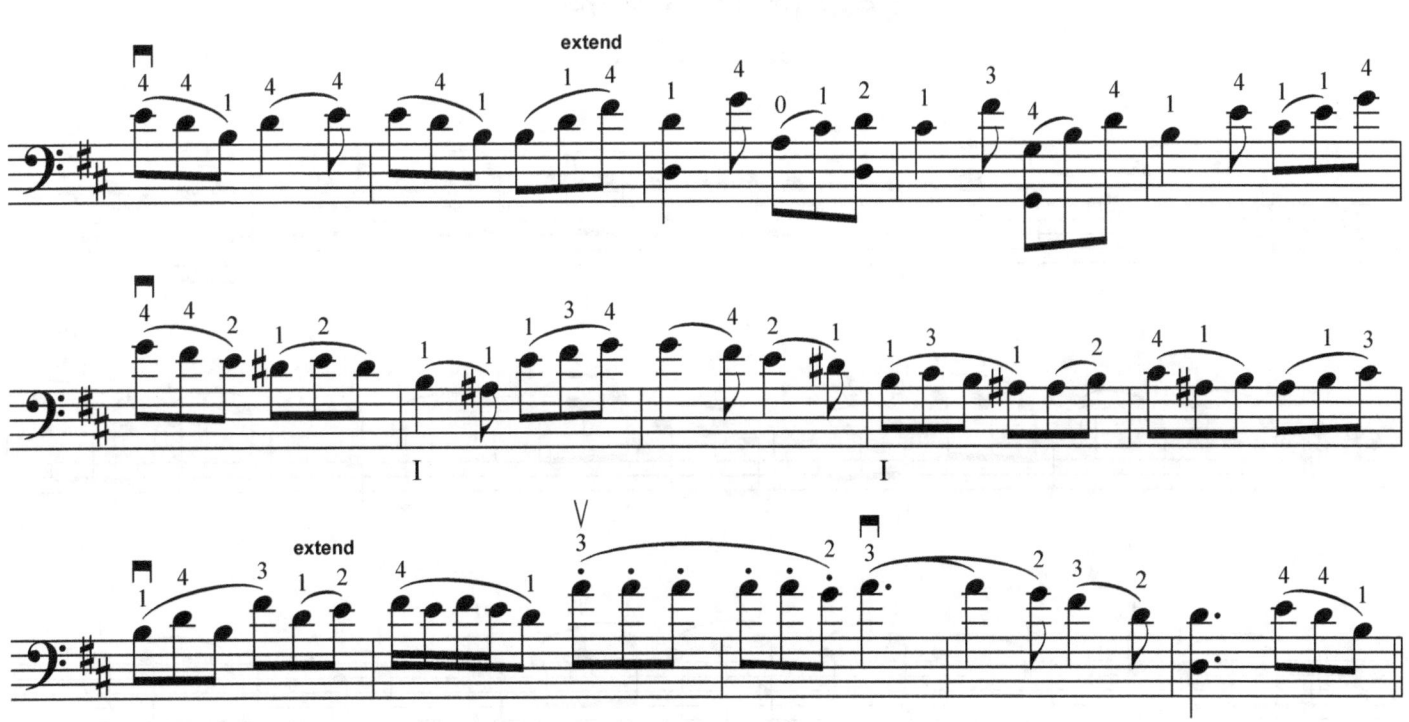

©2020 C. Harvey Publications All Rights Reserved.

78 The Goltermann Concerto No. 4 Study Book for Cello

Learning the Notes I
Measures 31-36

Learning the Notes II
Measures 34-37

©2020 C. Harvey Publications   All Rights Reserved.

Positions Study: Measures 32-40

Shifting Across Strings: Measures 35-40

Concerto, Second Movement
Section Two: Measures 42-65a

Definitions

con anima: with spirit *dolce*: sweetly *cresc.*: gradually increase the volume

The Goltermann Concerto No. 4 Study Book for Cello 81

Introduction to B Major

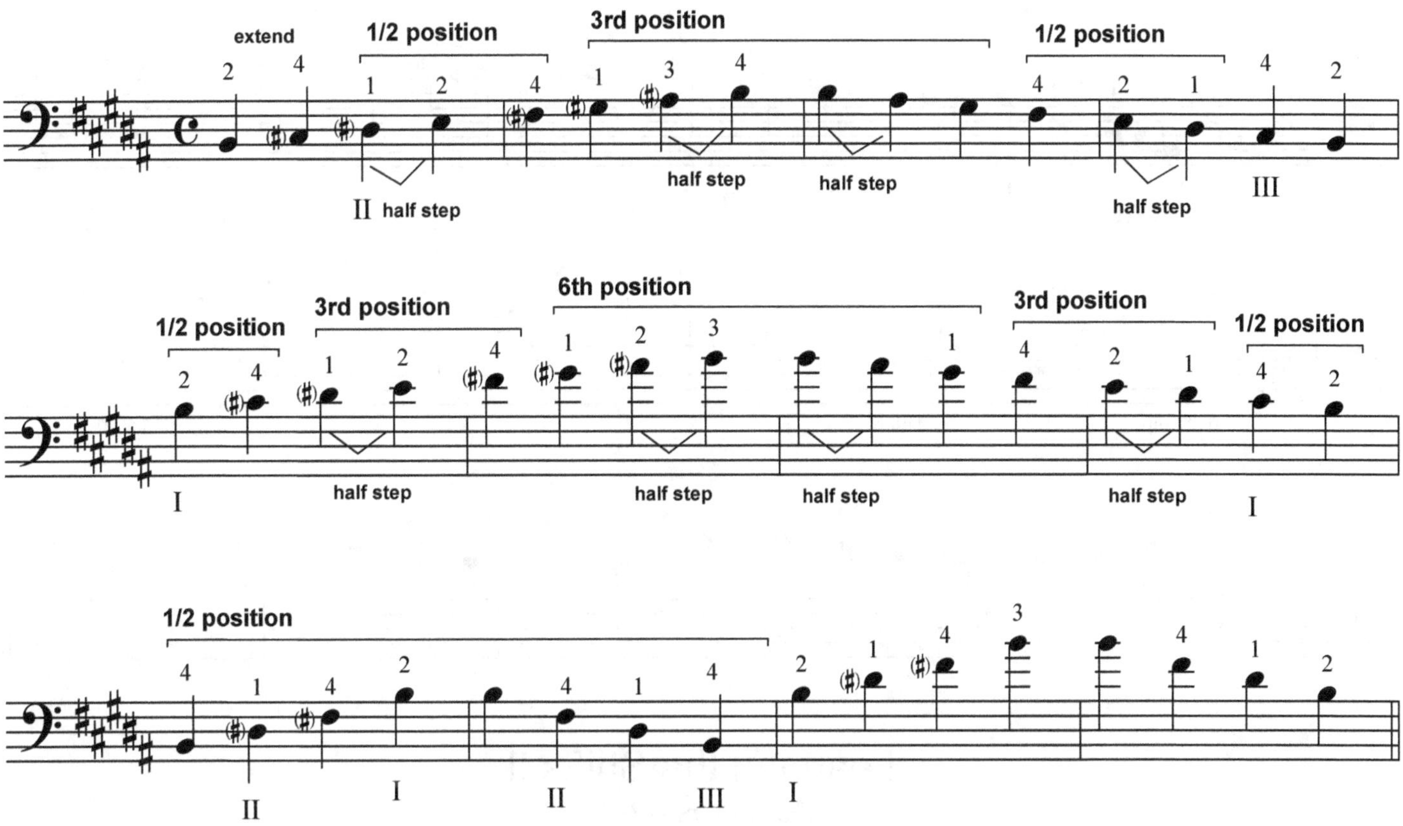

Learning the Notes
Measures 42-43

©2020 C. Harvey Publications All Rights Reserved.

Learning the Shifts I
Measures 43-44

Learning the Shifts II
Measures 42-48

The Goltermann Concerto No. 4 Study Book for Cello

Rhythm and Bowing
Measures 42-49

Shifting I
Measures 50-52

©2020 C. Harvey Publications   All Rights Reserved.

Shifting II: Measures 53-56

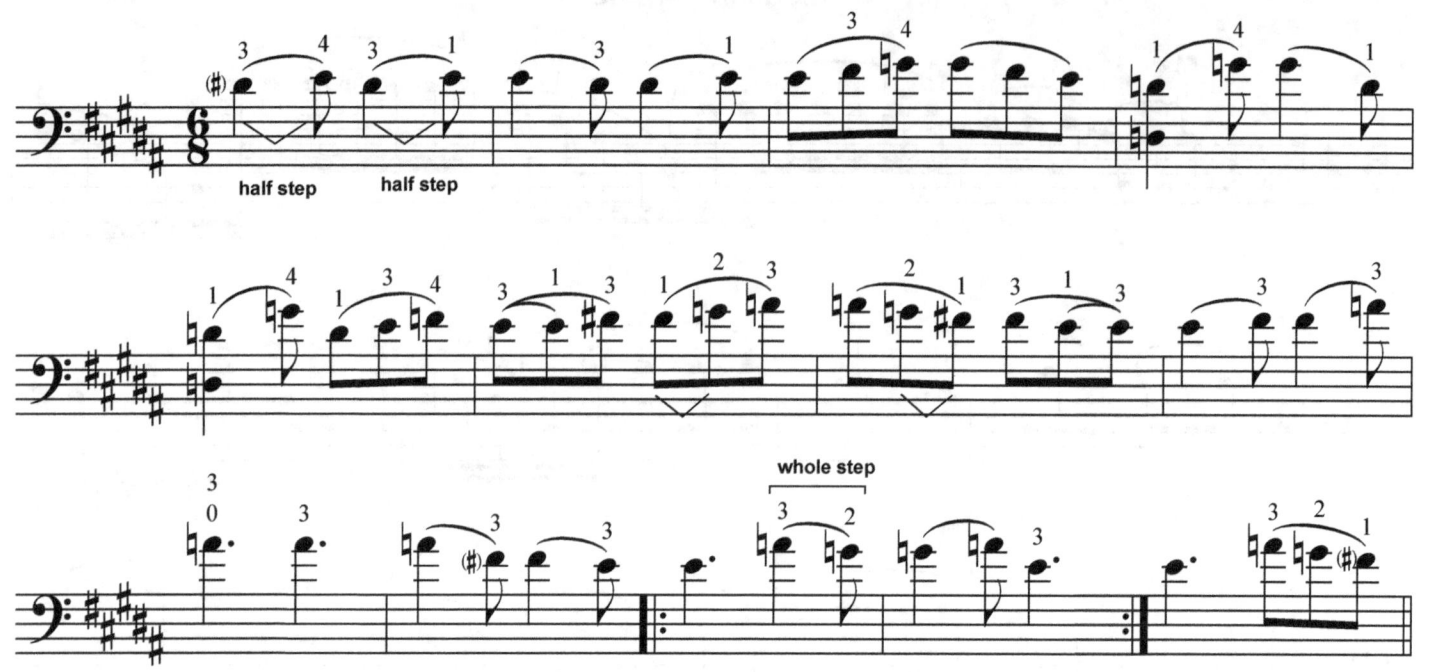

Shifting III: Measures 56-60

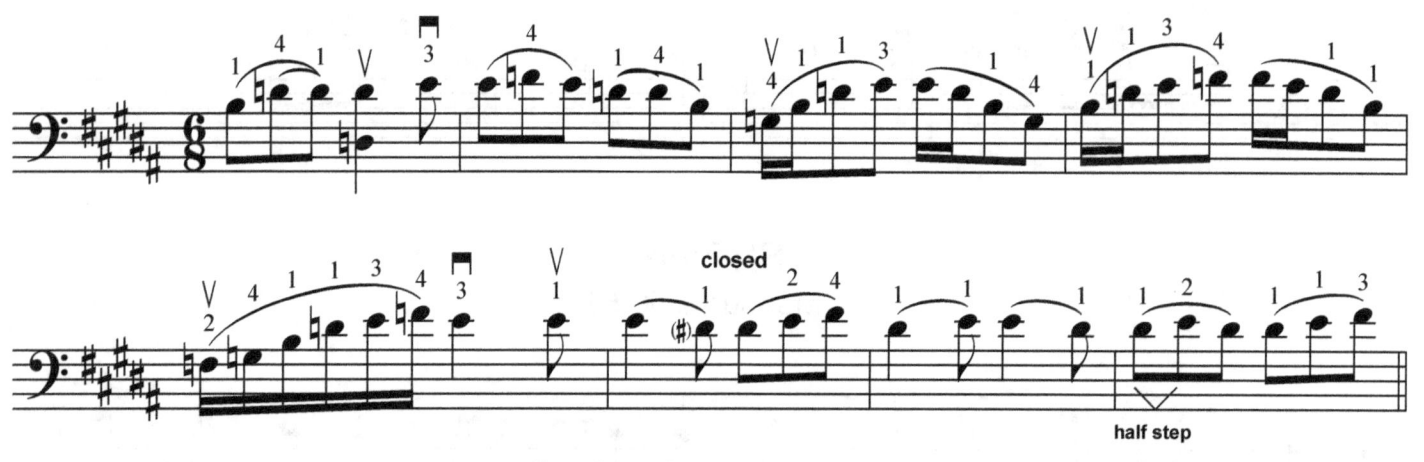

Bowing: Measure 56

Learning the Notes
Measures 57-60

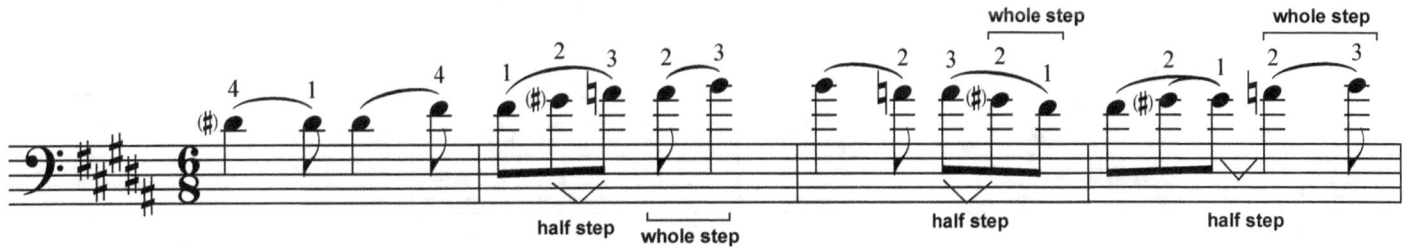

Sixth Position: Measures 61-65a

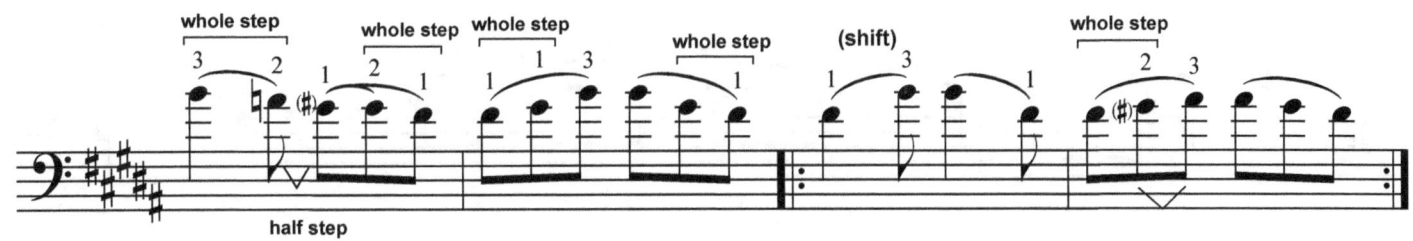

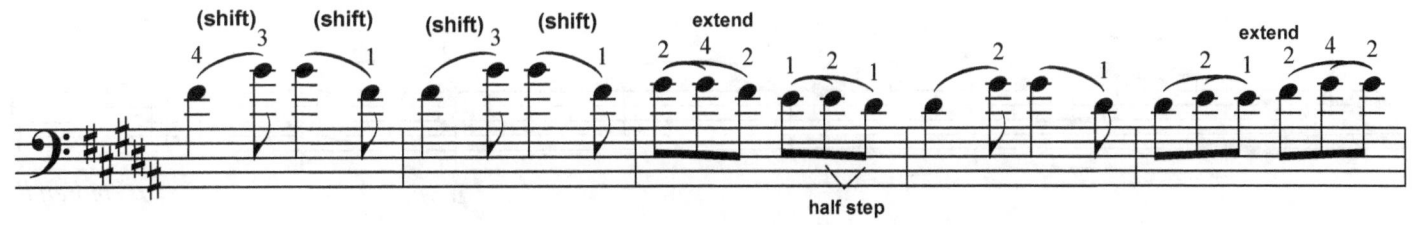

Concerto, Second Movement
Section Three: Measures 65-92 (end of movement)

Definitions
dim: gradually decrease the volume
cresc.: gradually increase the volume
morendo: decrease in volume and tempo to make the sound die away

The Goltermann Concerto No. 4 Study Book for Cello 87

©2020 C. Harvey Publications All Rights Reserved.

88

The Goltermann Concerto No. 4 Study Book for Cello

Exercises for measures 73-89 are found on pages 72-77, as these measures were repeated.

Shifting Review I: Measures 5-40

Shifting Review II: Measures 5-40

©2020 C. Harvey Publications All Rights Reserved.

The Goltermann Concerto No. 4 Study Book for Cello

Concerto, Third Movement
Section One: Measures 13-32

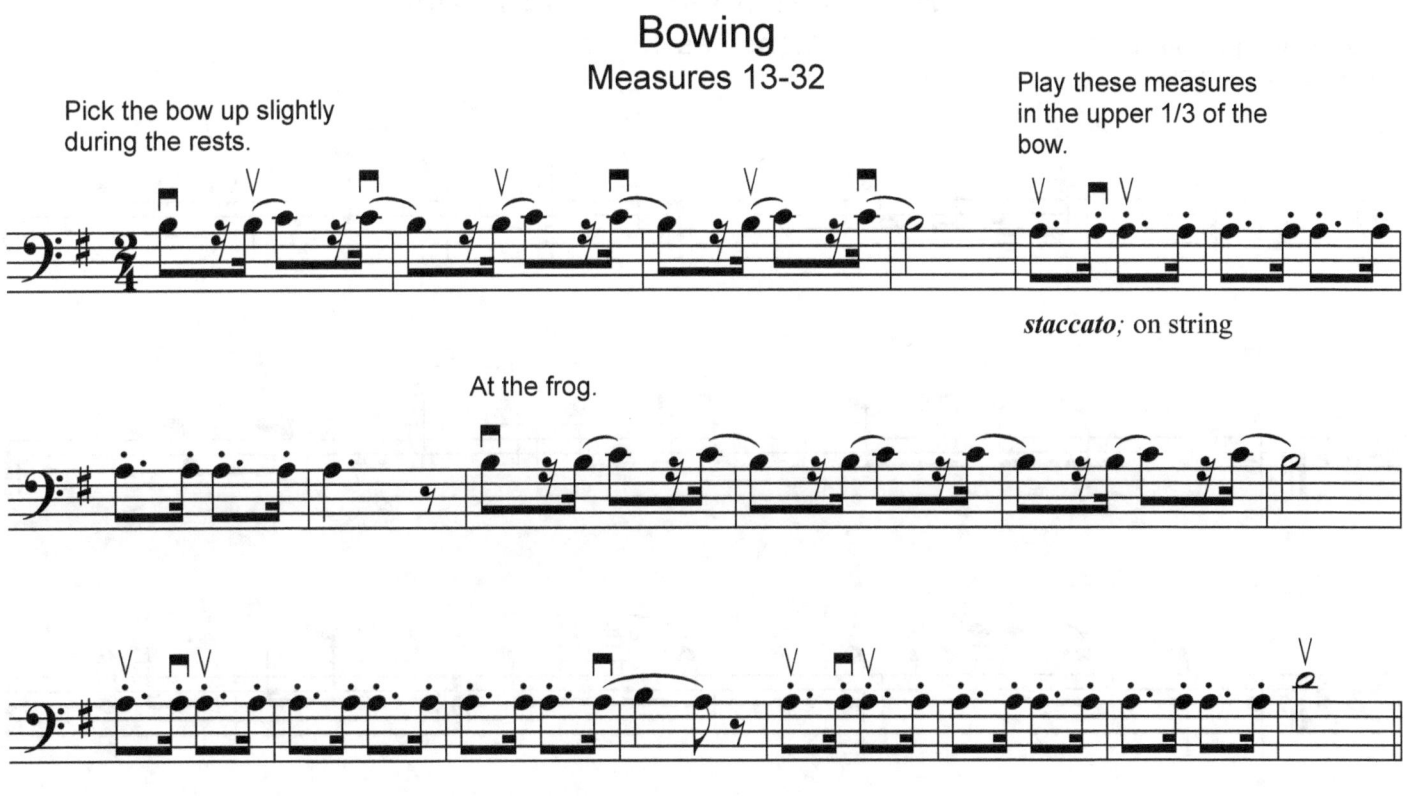

Definitions
leggiero con grazia: lightly, gracefully

marcato: a heavy, marked staccato

Bowing
Measures 13-32

Pick the bow up slightly during the rests.

Play these measures in the upper 1/3 of the bow.

staccato; on string

At the frog.

©2020 C. Harvey Publications All Rights Reserved.

Concerto, Third Movement, Section Two: Measures 33-72

Definitions
marcato: a heavy, marked staccato   *cresc.*: gradually increase the volume

Shifting I
Measures 33-39

Shifting II
Measures 37-44

©2020 C. Harvey Publications   All Rights Reserved.

The Goltermann Concerto No. 4 Study Book for Cello 93

Bowing: Measures 43-48

Finger Exercise: Measures 49-60

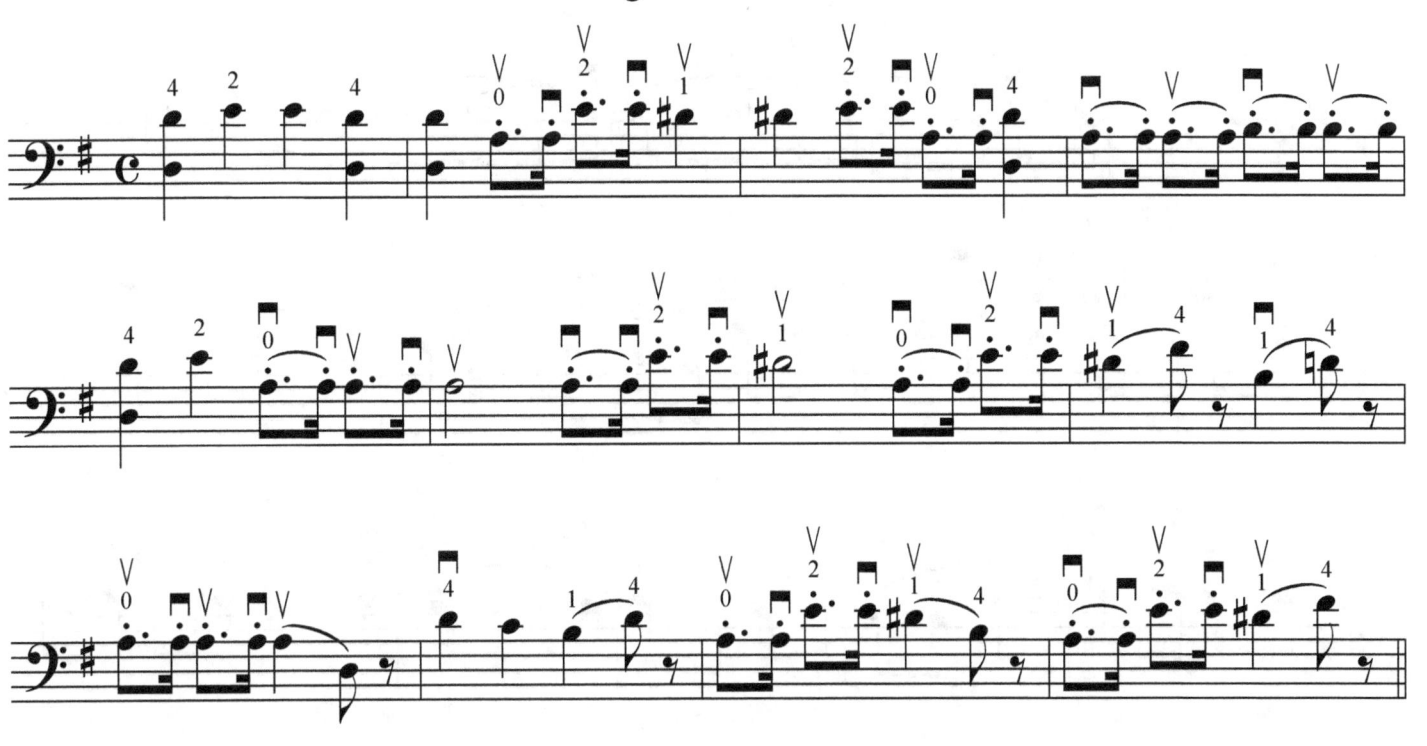

Repeat several times, playing faster each time.

©2020 C. Harvey Publications All Rights Reserved.

Hooked Bowing I: Measures 61-64

Hooked Bowing II: Measures 61-72

Concerto, Third Movement
Section Three: Measures 96-112

Shifting I: Measures 96-100

Shifting II
Measures 100-112

The Goltermann Concerto No. 4 Study Book for Cello 97

Shifting III
Measures 106-112

Bowing
Measures 96-112

©2020 C. Harvey Publications   All Rights Reserved.

Concerto, Third Movement
Section Four: Measures 116-159

Definitions
molto grazioso e affettuoso: very gracefully and tenderly
con fuoco: in a fiery manner
pesante: heavy
cresc.: gradually increase the volume
rallent.: gradually decrease the speed

©2020 C. Harvey Publications All Rights Reserved.

The Goltermann Concerto No. 4 Study Book for Cello 99

Shifting: Measures 116-127

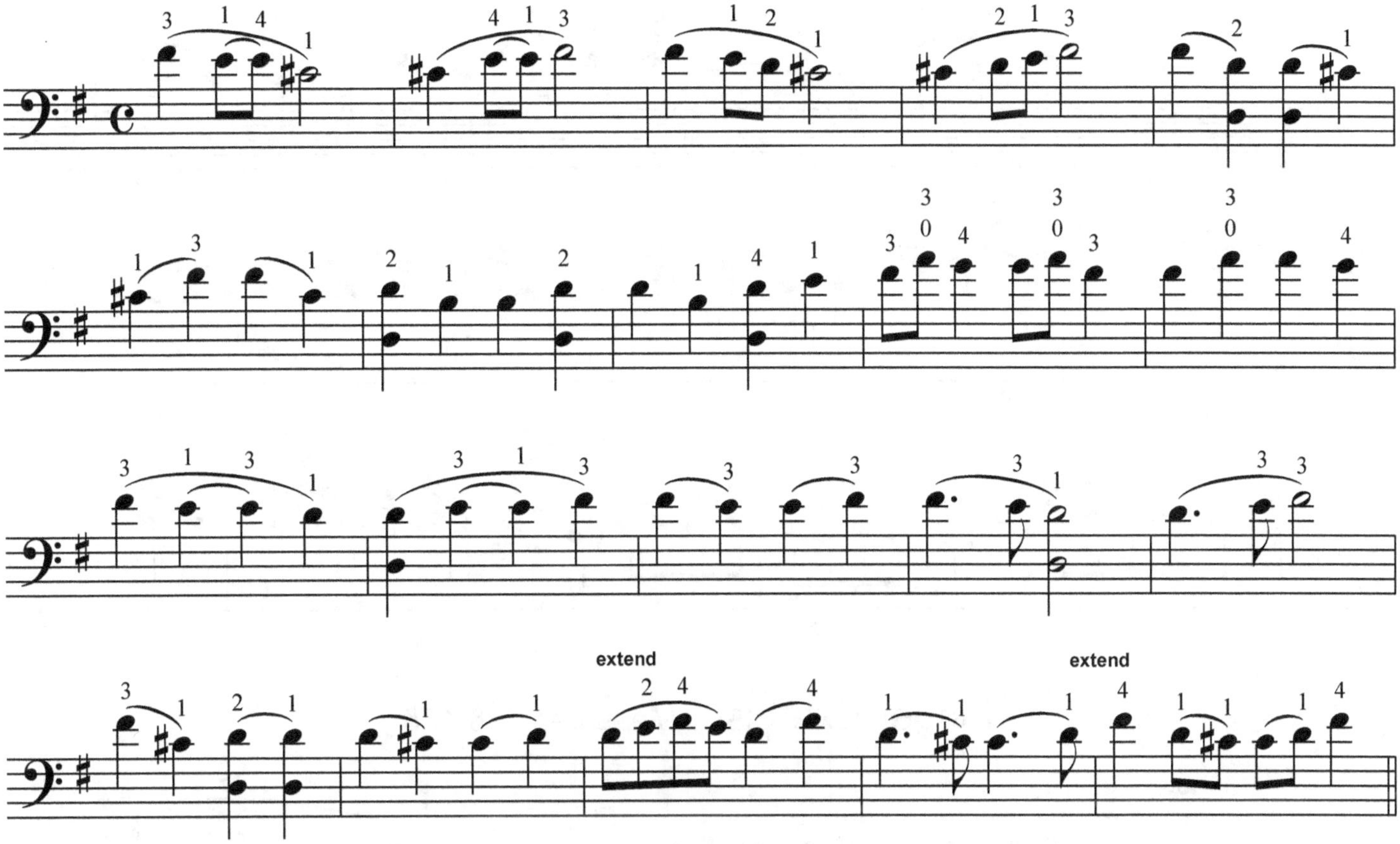

Learning the Notes I: Measures 126-129

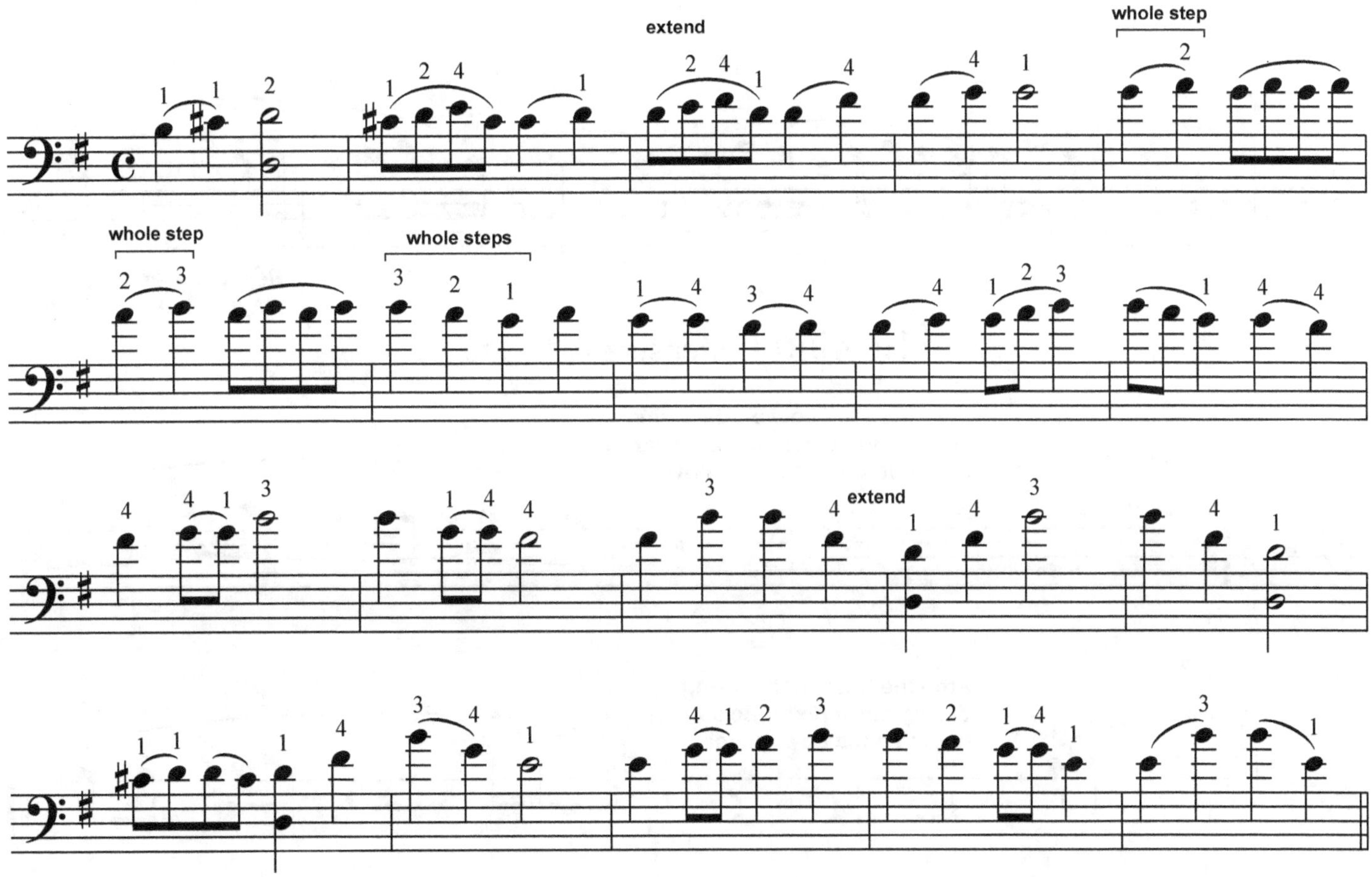

©2020 C. Harvey Publications All Rights Reserved.

Learning the Notes II: Measures 130-137

Finger Exercise: Measures 128-135

Repeat several times, playing faster each time.

Bowing I: Measures 116-119

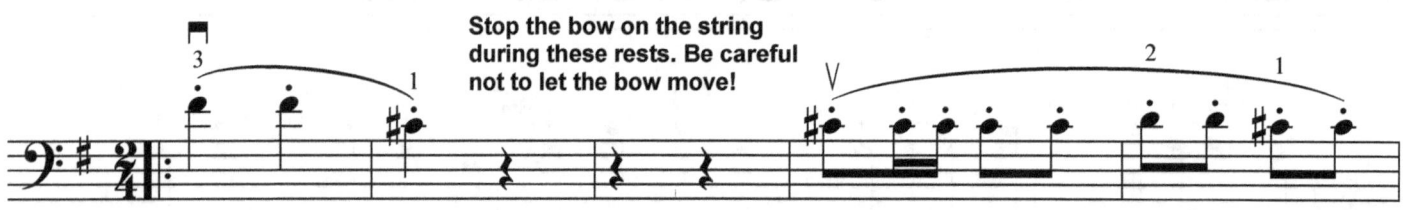

Stop the bow on the string during these rests. Be careful not to let the bow move!

Stop the bow on the string during these rests. Be careful not to let the bow move!

The Goltermann Concerto No. 4 Study Book for Cello

Bowing II: Measures 120-137

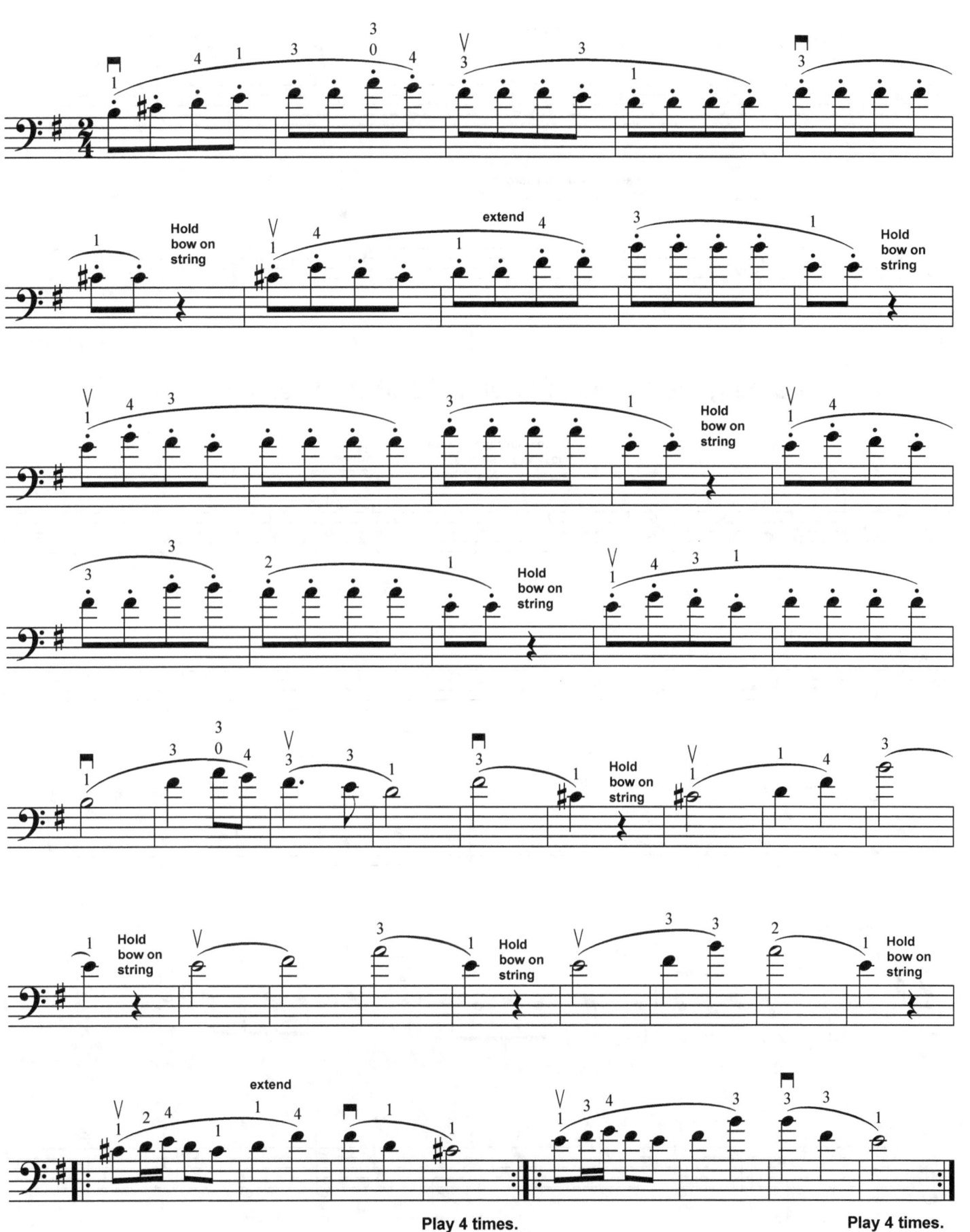

Shifting to the Thumb: Measure 139

Play 4 times.

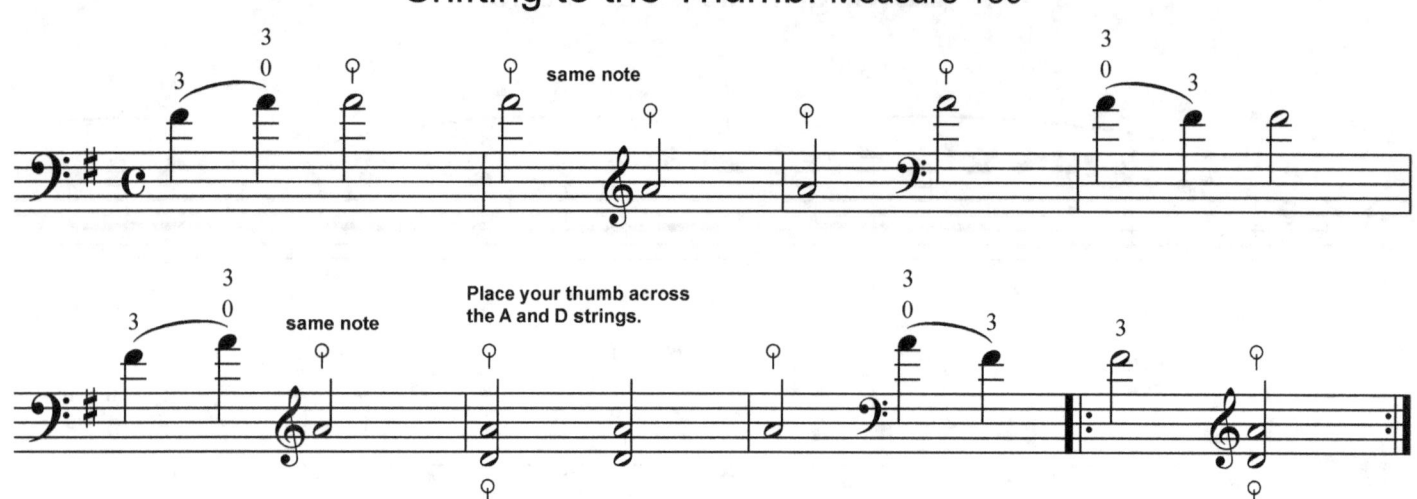

Learning the Notes in Thumb Position: Measures 139-143

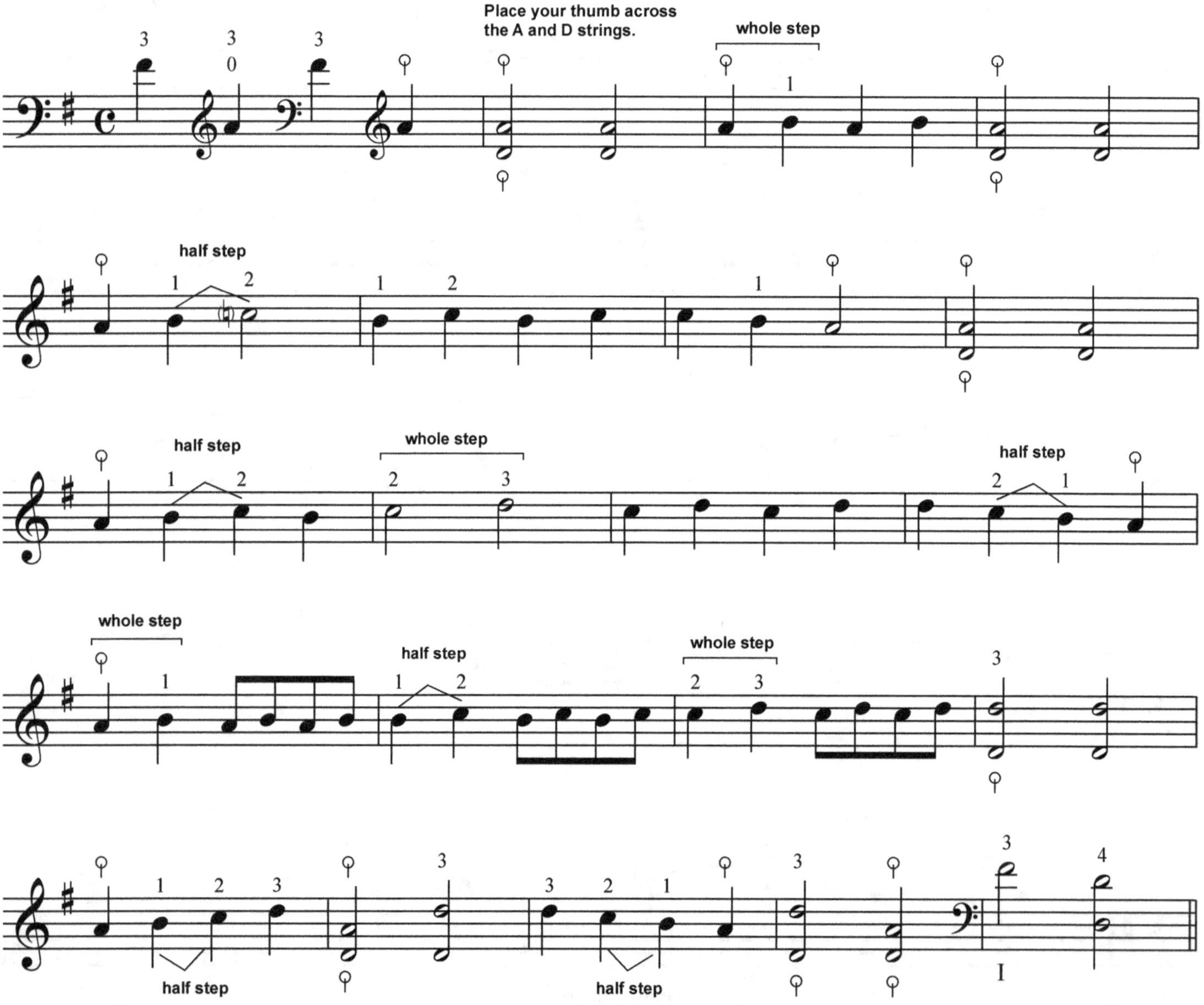

The Goltermann Concerto No. 4 Study Book for Cello

Shifting Into Thumb Position In a Long Slur: Measures 138-141

Playing in Thumb Position: Measures 136-144

©2020 C. Harvey Publications All Rights Reserved.

Concerto, Third Movement
Section Five: Measures 160-196

Definitions
spiccato: a light bowing that bounces off the string; see page 106.

How Spiccato Works

Because both the bow hair and the string are flexibly stretched, the bow can bounce on the string. By relaxing your arm and hand and timing the bounce correctly, you can get a very good spiccato sound.

Where to Play Spiccato

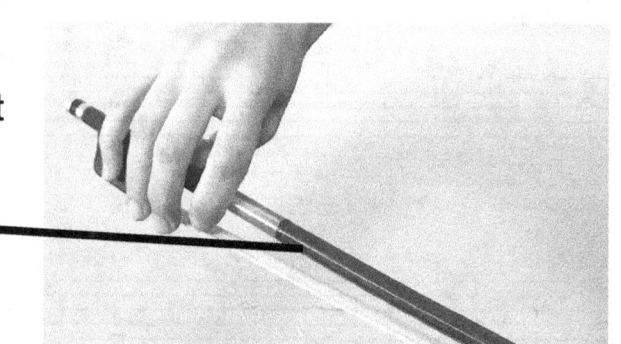

Bouncing is often easiest at the balance point of the bow, between where you hold the bow and the middle of the bow. This will vary from bow to bow.

On the string, spiccato works best when played near the fingerboard
(not near the bridge.)

Ideal Tempos for Spiccato

In 4/4 or 3/4 timing: ♩ = 100-120

In 6/8 timing: ♩. = 70-85

If the tempo is too slow, the bow will not bounce.

How to Practice Spiccato

- Since spiccato needs to be played at a fairly quick tempo in order to work, **start learning spiccato on repeated notes.**
- Start practicing on open strings and then **try spiccato on predictable patterns such as scales.**
- Whenever you are having difficulty with a spiccato passage, **focus on the string crossings**, which can often cause trouble.

Shifting and Feeling Triplets
Measures 46-47

Repeat several times, playing faster each time.

Spiccato Study No. 1

Spiccato Study No. 2

The Goltermann Concerto No. 4 Study Book for Cello

Learning the Notes I: Measures 184-194

Learning the Notes II: Measures 188-196

Note: See pages 65-66 to see where these notes are on the fingerboard.

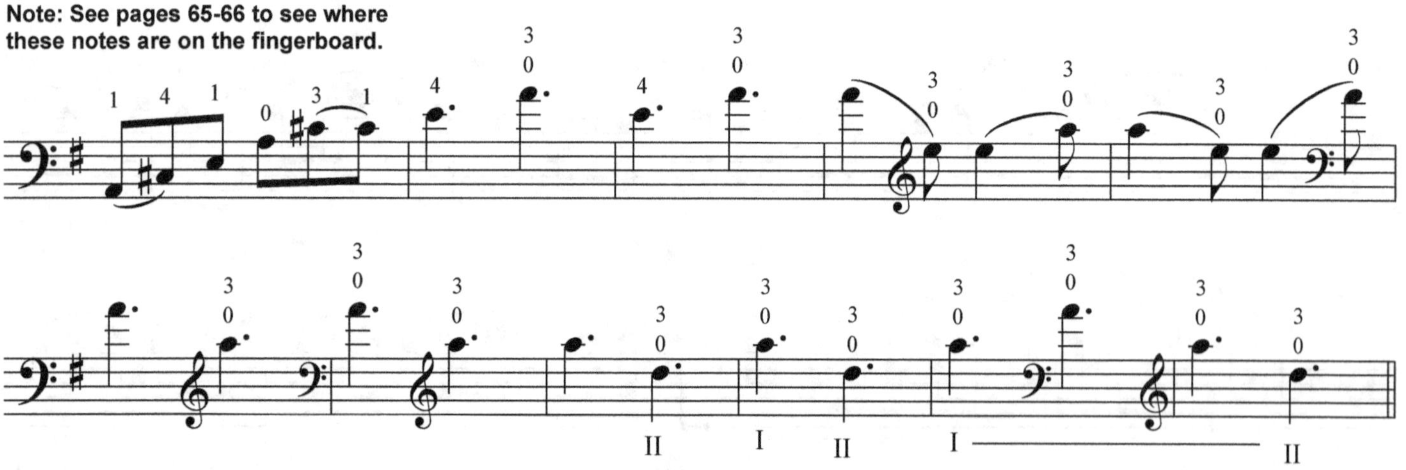

©2020 C. Harvey Publications All Rights Reserved.

Concerto, Third Movement: Section Six: Measures 217-284

Learning the Notes: Measures 217-224

Note: Measures 225-284 are identical to measures 13-72. See pages 89-94 for work on these measures.

Concerto, Third Movement
Section Seven: Measures 308-324

©2020 C. Harvey Publications All Rights Reserved.

The Goltermann Concerto No. 4 Study Book for Cello
113

Mapping the Positions I: Measures 308-315

Mapping the Positions II: Measures 316-320

©2020 C. Harvey Publications All Rights Reserved.

Shifting Exercise I: Measures 308-324

Shifting Exercise II: Measures 308-324

The Goltermann Concerto No. 4 Study Book for Cello

Fluency Exercise: Measures 308-324

Bowing: Measures 311-321

©2020 C. Harvey Publications   All Rights Reserved.

The Goltermann Concerto No. 4 Study Book for Cello   117

Shifting I: Measures 328-341

Shifting II: Measures 340-355

©2020 C. Harvey Publications   All Rights Reserved.

Finger Exercise
Measures 338-339, 354-355

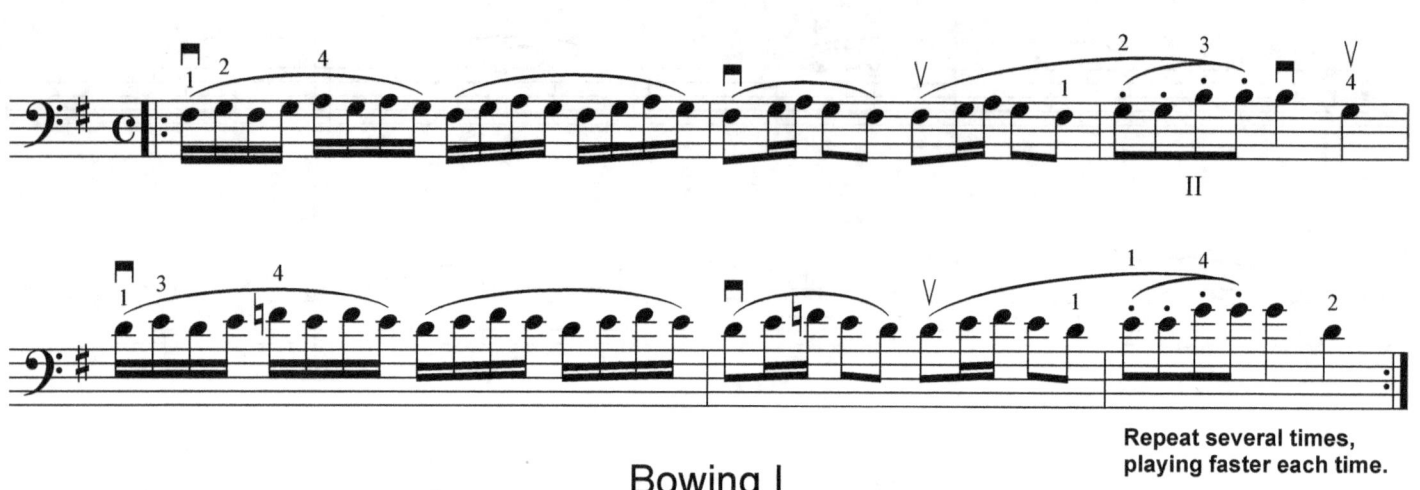

Repeat several times, playing faster each time.

Bowing I
Measures 328-331

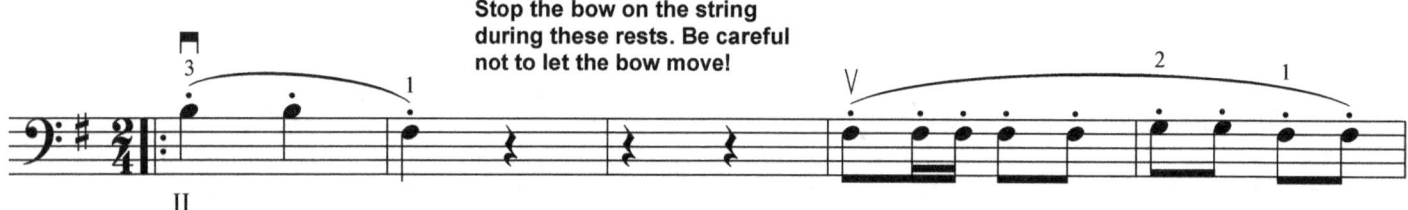

Stop the bow on the string during these rests. Be careful not to let the bow move!

Stop the bow on the string during these rests. Be careful not to let the bow move!

Bowing II
Measures 332-355

Hold bow on string

Hold bow on string

©2020 C. Harvey Publications All Rights Reserved.

The Goltermann Concerto No. 4 Study Book for Cello 119

Bowing III
Measures 328-355

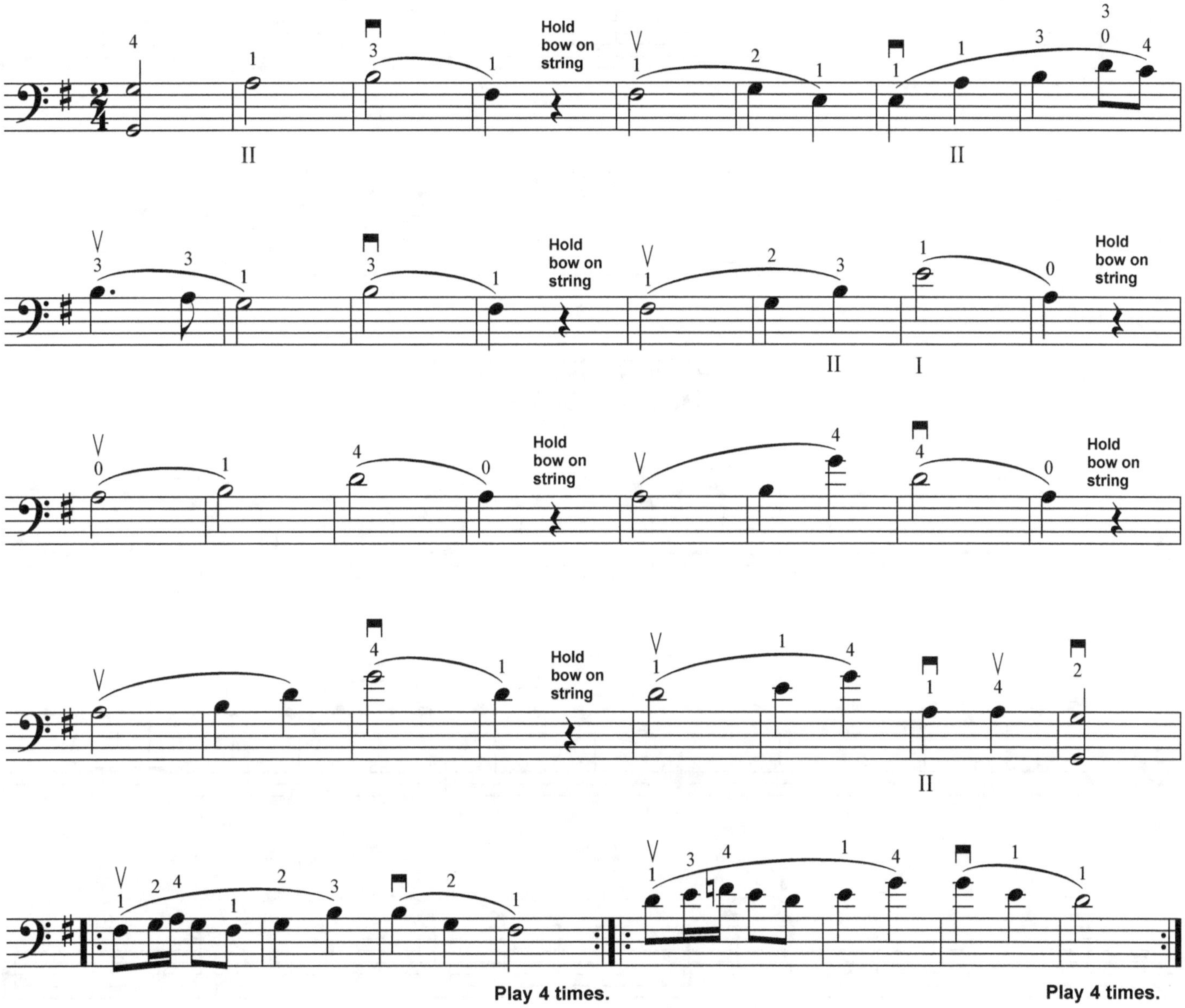

Play 4 times.   Play 4 times.

©2020 C. Harvey Publications All Rights Reserved.

Learning the Notes I
Measures 356-362

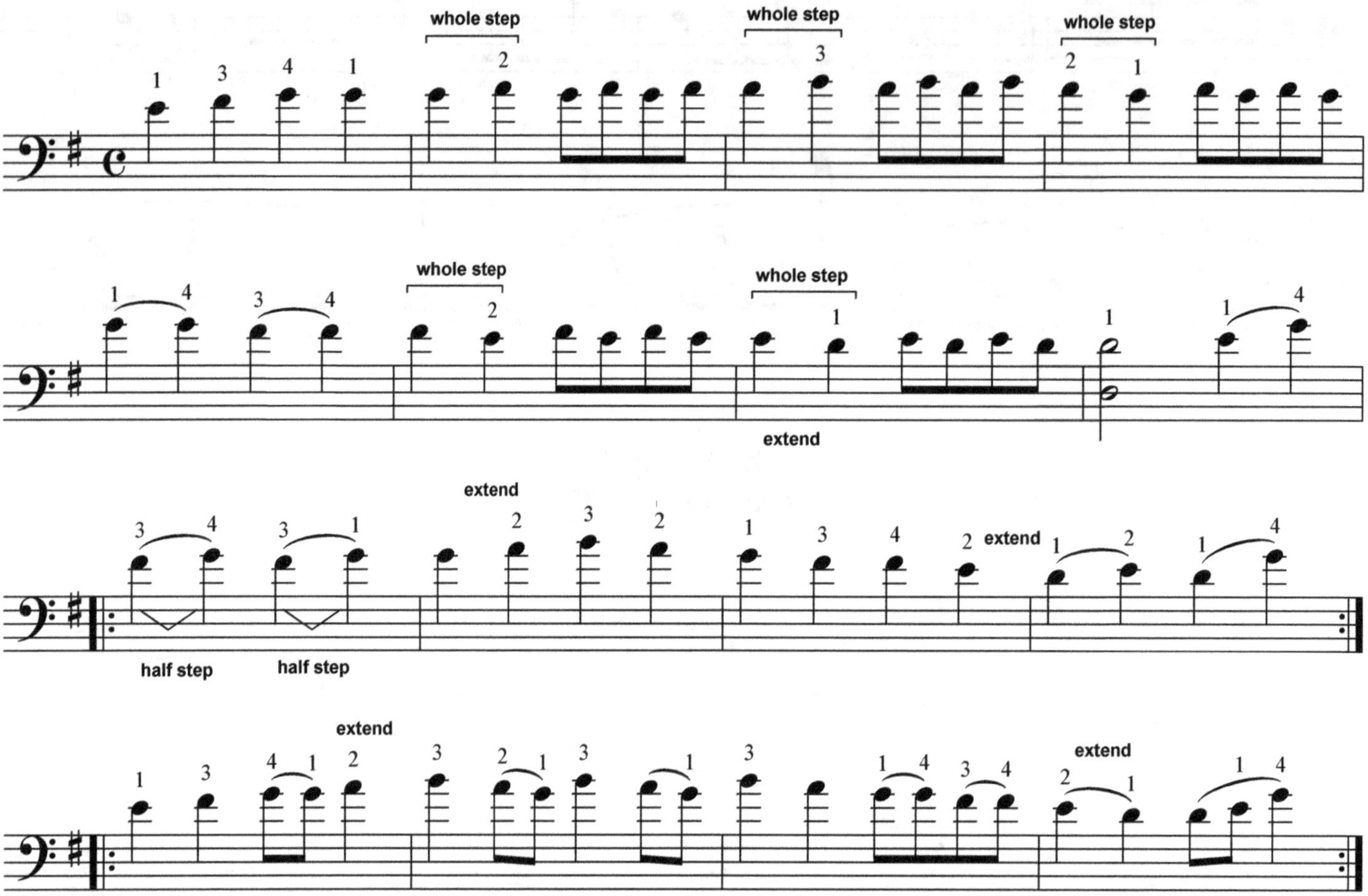

Learning the Notes II
Measures 356-362

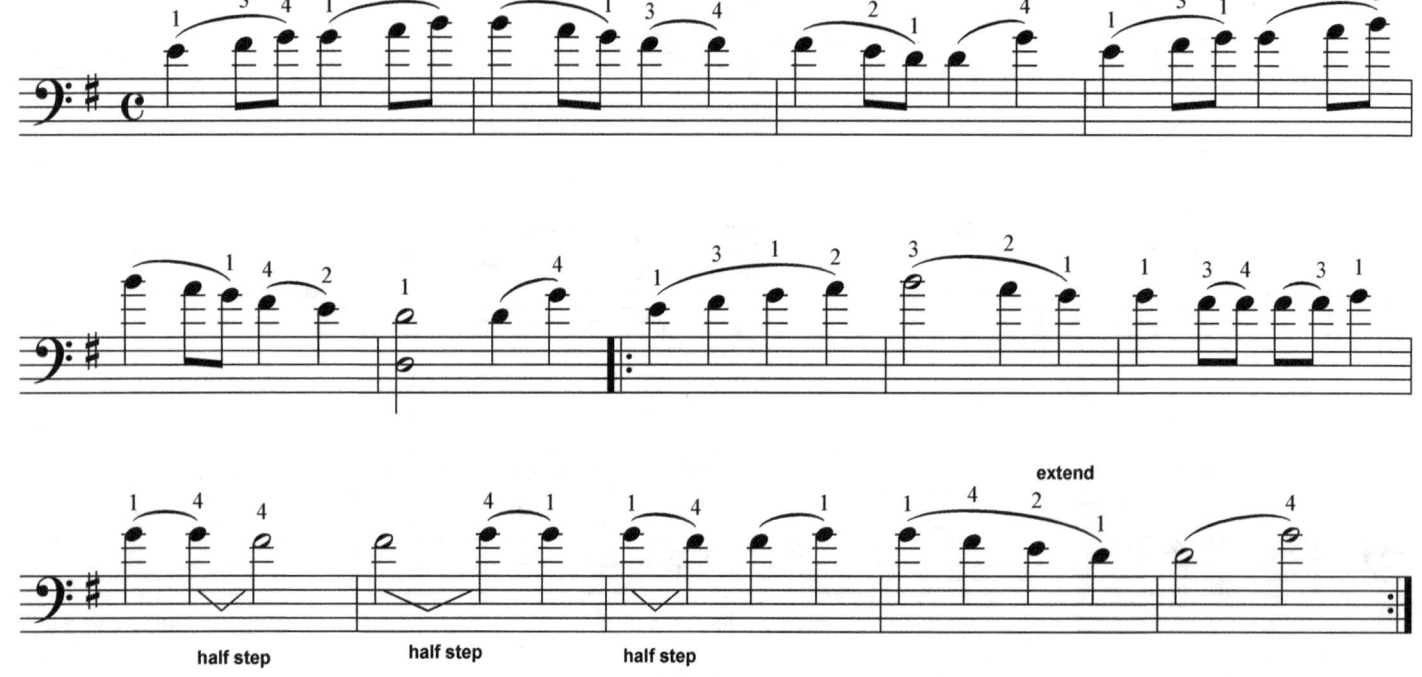

The Goltermann Concerto No. 4 Study Book for Cello

Learning the Notes, Top Fingering: Measures 363-371

Learning the Notes, Bottom Fingering: Measures 363-371

©2020 C. Harvey Publications All Rights Reserved.

Concerto, Third Movement
Section Nine: Measures 372-411

Definitions
spiccato: a light bowing that bounces off the string; see page 104. *cresc.:* gradually increase the volume
pesante: heavy   *dim.:* gradually decrease the volume

Shifting and Feeling Triplets
Measures 372-387

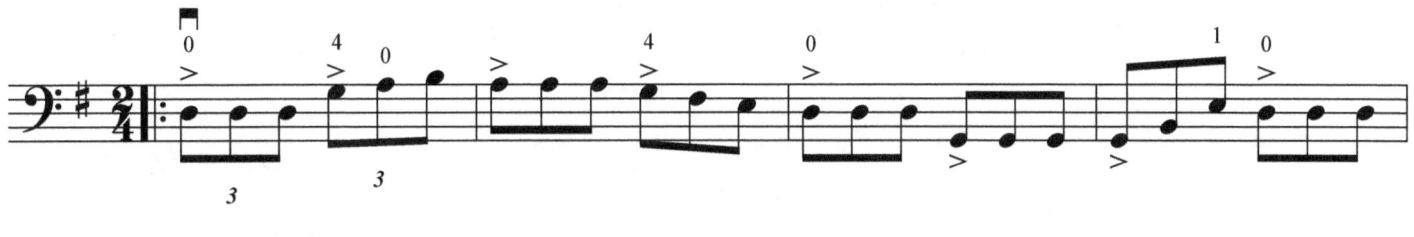

Repeat several times, playing faster each time.

Spiccato Study I

Spiccato Study II

Spiccato Study III

Spiccato Bowing I: Measures 376-379

The Goltermann Concerto No. 4 Study Book for Cello

©2020 C. Harvey Publications All Rights Reserved.

Learning the Notes II: Measures 388-395

Forming the Arpeggios I: Measures 388-395

The Goltermann Concerto No. 4 Study Book for Cello

Forming the Arpeggios II: Measures 388-395

Bowing I: Measures 388-395

Bowing II: Measures 388-395

Bowing III: Measures 388-395

staccato; on string

Repeat several times, playing faster each time.

©2020 C. Harvey Publications All Rights Reserved.

Double Stops for Reaching Across Strings: Measures 388-395

Fluency: Measures 388-395

The Goltermann Concerto No. 4 Study Book for Cello

Learning the Bowing: Measures 396-401

Repeat several times, playing faster each time.

Learning the Notes I: Measures 396-403

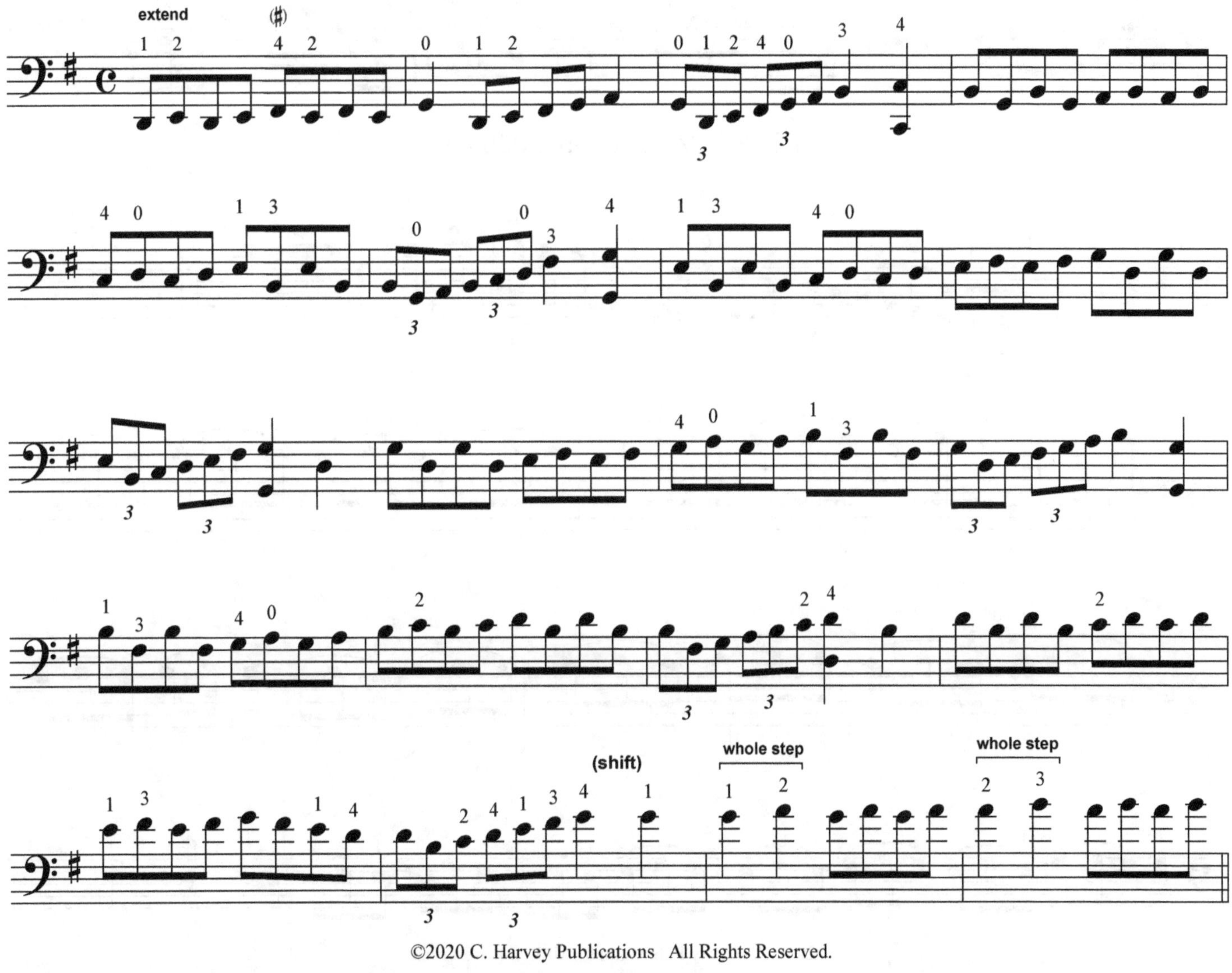

©2020 C. Harvey Publications   All Rights Reserved.

Learning the Notes II: Measures 402-411

Fluency: Measures 396-411

The Goltermann Concerto No. 4 Study Book for Cello   131

Concerto, Third Movement: Section Ten: Measures 412-459 (end)

Definitions
Piu animato: with more animation
sempre f: play consistently forte
cresc.: gradually increase the volume
brillante: brilliantly, with sparkle

©2020 C. Harvey Publications All Rights Reserved.

Learning the Notes: Measures 412-426

Learning How Far to Shift: Measures 412-426

©2020 C. Harvey Publications All Rights Reserved.

The Goltermann Concerto No. 4 Study Book for Cello

Putting the Arpeggios Together: Measures 412-426

Stringing the Shifts Together: Measures 412-426

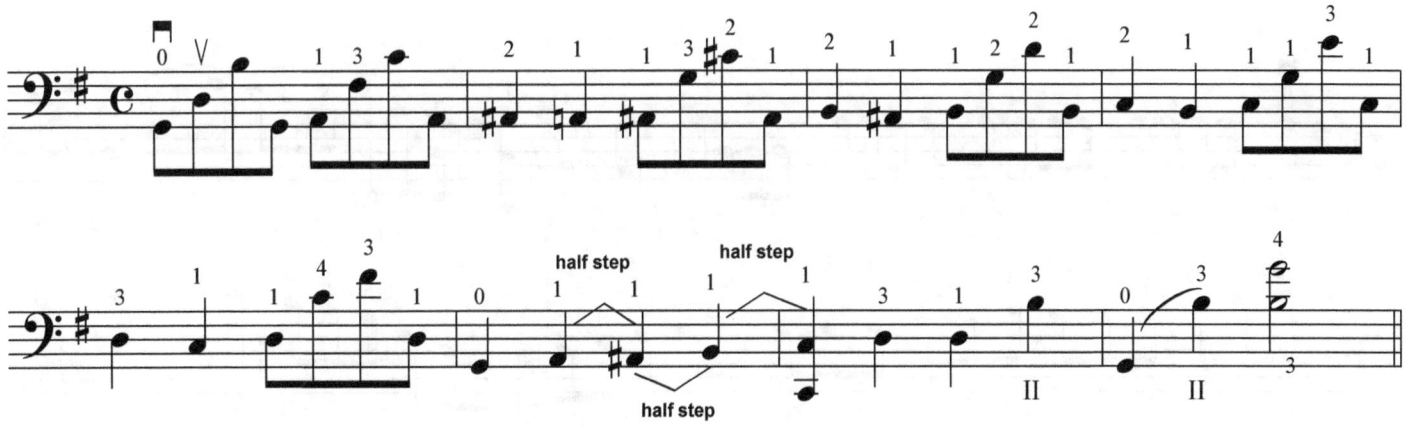

©2020 C. Harvey Publications All Rights Reserved.

Fluency: Measures 412-426

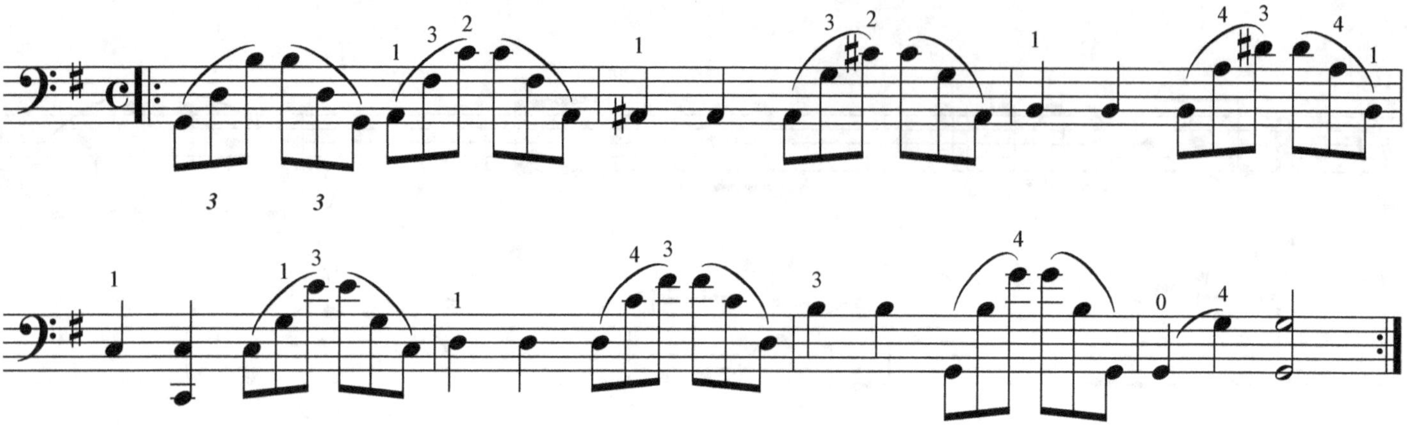

Learning the Notes, Top Fingering
Measures 426-433

Agility II: Measures 439-442

Repeat several times, playing faster each time.

Learning the Notes: Measures 443-459

The Goltermann Concerto No. 4 Study Book for Cello

Fluency: Measures 443-459

Chords: Measures 454-459

©2020 C. Harvey Publications All Rights Reserved.

Concerto No. 4 in G Major

G. Goltermann
Edited by C. Harvey

The Goltermann Cello Concerto No. 4 Study Book - Complete Piece

The Goltermann Cello Concerto No. 4 Study Book - Complete Piece 141

The Goltermann Cello Concerto No. 4 Study Book - Complete Piece

The Goltermann Cello Concerto No. 4 Study Book - Complete Piece
145

The Goltermann Cello Concerto No. 4 Study Book - Complete Piece   147

148 The Goltermann Cello Concerto No. 4 Study Book - Complete Piece

www.ingramcontent.com/pod-product-compliance
Lightning Source LLC
Chambersburg PA
CBHW081113080526

44587CB00021B/3576